W9-BWE-480

It Comes with the Territory

ALSO BY ANNE M. TURNER
AND FROM MCFARLAND

Vote Yes for Libraries:
A Guide to Winning Ballot Measure
Campaigns for Library Funding (2000)

It Comes with the Territory

Handling Problem Situations in Libraries

REVISED EDITION

Anne M. Turner

with a foreword by
Gordon Conable

McFarland & Company, Inc., Publishers
Jefferson, North Carolina, and London

To Steve, for all the love,
for all the years,
and to the staff,
past and present, of the
Santa Cruz City County Library System

Library of Congress Cataloguing-in-Publication Data

Turner, Anne M., 1941–
It comes with the territory :
handling problem situations in libraries /
Anne M. Turner; with a foreword by Gordon Conable.—
Revised ed.
p.   cm.
Includes bibliographical references and index.

ISBN 0-7864-1887-7 (softcover : 50# alkaline paper)

1. Public services (Libraries).
2. Libraries and people with social disabilities.
3. Library rules and regulations.
4. Libraries and community.   I. Title.
Z711.T873   2004   025.5—dc22   2004008631

British Library cataloguing data are available

Cover photograph ©2004 Corbis Images

Manufactured in the United States of America

*McFarland & Company, Inc., Publishers
Box 611, Jefferson, North Carolina 28640
www.mcfarlandpub.com*

Table of Contents

Foreword to the Second Edition

Gordon Conable

There's the stuff they teach in library school, and then there's the stuff that comes along that you never imagined you'd find yourself dealing with:

The marathon runner flaked out on a bench in the lobby, snoring, his running shorts hiked up and a gentle breeze caressing portions of his exposed anatomy that should never be publicly presented.

The newspaper reporter shouting at the librarian (who has just politely informed her that her time on the public PC has expired), announcing that she is on deadline and has a greater need for the machine than the kid who is scheduled to use the computer and has a heavy date in a chat room.

The woman who wants all the encyclopedia volumes arranged on the floor in front of her before going to the index.

The family living in the rusted van in the library parking lot.

The man with the seeing-eye ferret.

And what's that enticing smell of barbecue wafting out of the rest room?

The first edition of this book provided a witty, thoughtful approach to a wide range of issues involving the behavior of patrons in libraries and what to do about it. This time it's even better.

The constant in library work is that whenever you think you've seen it all, along comes a situation that is mind-bogglingly new. I've been working in libraries for almost thirty years, yet every week I encounter some situation that amazes, challenges, sometimes amuses, but isn't quite like anything that's happened before. Sometimes these situations are fraught with peril, including the peril of liability. Sometimes they're incredibly irritating. Sometimes they're willfully constructed to push our buttons and confront the institution in ways that demand deft and nimble responses—expecially when no one on duty feels particularly nimble or deft at the moment.

I've seen libraries with policies and procedural manuals that seem to get thicker by inches every month. They contain detailed instructions on how to respond to the new unique situation that flummoxed some staff member just last week—or, given how long it takes to promulgate and vet these things, just last year or the year before that. And then there are all the forms to report them. These endless tomes of rules become security blankets, huge bureaucratic weights upon our operational conscience, and massive traps if, heaven help us, we inadvertently violate one of their precepts the next time someone starts cooking with a hibachi in the men's room.

If you want to find out how to develop manuals of this kind, this book is not for you.

But if you'd like a fresh, tart approach to the kind of rules that actually work, the kind of responses that address the gnarly circumstances that arise because the people who use libraries will *always* foil our expectations, you'll find help here. If you're looking for ways to balance professional values and principles with legal requirements and user friendly service, this'll get you thinking.

If you want to encourage better judgment and less panicky responses from your eager (but sometimes beleaguered) staff and colleagues, this book will stimulate useful conversation.

Anne Turner has opinions and expresses them. She also has deep respect for the learning process, and nothing seems to ruffle her unnecessarily. *It Comes with the Territory* is a practical, knowledgeable guide to dealing with behavioral problems that occur in libraries. Turner offers immensely useful guidance about writing good, clear policies and procedures.

Turner describes difficult problems and suggests approaches that do not compromise professional ethics or principles. She talks about complicated legal issues in straightforward, understandable language. In these pages you will find support, assistance, and legal backing for wading in and coping when angels hold back and where fools fear to tread. There is good material here for staff training and lots of food for thought.

This edition contains new material addressing issues (like the Internet) that weren't really challenging us in the same way a decade ago. The revision and expansion of this classic illustrates the cumulative understanding of human behavior that comes from reflections on an additional wealth of unpredictable experience accumulated since the first edition.

When confronting challenging situations, it is essential to use approaches that do not needlessly cause minor problems to escalate into major ones. That principle, and the principle that the rights of each library user must be protected against needless restriction—and protected from interference in their exercise by the problems presented by other library users—are twin threads that consistently inform Turner's approach.

This is not your standard, dry professional volume. If you live in libraries as they really are, you'll find a great deal of good sense herein, a lot to recognize, and a lot you can use to improve your library, your approach to behavior problems, and your attitude about these things.

As the physician first seeks to do no harm, the librarian must first seek to impose no limits on the exercise of intellectual freedom and free expression. This is all easier said than done. But Anne Turner's book should make it easier to do it well.

Gordon Conable has been employed in public libraries since the 1970s. He has worked in bookmobiles and on the reference desk, been a library director, and spent decades in the trenches of censorship battles and First Amendment issues involving libraries. "Once I thought I had seen it all; now I know I haven't and need books like this one to help me keep my perspective."

Preface

My, how times change. Back in 1992, when I first worked on *It Comes with the Territory*, we librarians were terribly concerned about our behavior rules, mostly the ones about hygiene and dress. The *Kreimer v. Morristown* case, in which a homeless man challenged a public library's rules on First Amendment grounds, was decided in the library's favor. But many of us were unhappy with the disjunction between the popular perception of public libraries exhibited by the judges, and the reality of library life.

Ten years later, our attention has shifted to the Internet, blocking software, and all the changes in library service that have been provoked by the technological revolution. Once again, judges have weighed in with a dose of unreality ("Just turn the blocking software off," they say in the CIPA decision discussed in Chapter 7). And we librarians are left to cope. I hesitate to imagine what we may be discussing, thinking about, and endeavoring to fix a decade from now.

This revised edition of *It Comes with the Territory* has the same objective as the first. It is an effort to help librarians, especially those in middle and small size public libraries, develop behavior rules that work, and train staffs in how to implement them with fairness and reasonable humor. It assumes that the constituency of even the smallest public libraries is likely to be quite varied. It also assumes that because of this variety, problem situations will be frequent, and that ways must be found, regardless of problems, to do the library's job— delivering information services to the people.

It Comes with the Territory does not pretend to be a scholarly treatise. Rather, it tries to put together the best advice from librarians across the country, including me, based on our collective experiences. The new edition is divided into three parts. The first chapter is about writing behavior rules, and has been updated in the context of recent legal cases and First Amendment law. Chapters 2 through 7 discuss each category of problem behaviors with which most library staffs must deal. In every case the material has been updated. See especially a new section on creating a library workplace free of sexual harassment in Chapter 4, and a new Chapter 7 on Internet use. The final three chapters are on facilities security, writing staff manuals, and training staff.

Of course many people provided help and advice with both the first edition and this revision. Although I take full responsibility for the opinions expressed here, I owe them all a great debt for their contributions. I am particularly grateful to the current management staff of the Santa Cruz City County Library System: Susan Elgin, Gary Decker, Janis O'Driscoll, Margaret Souza, Dale Easley, and Barbara Gail Snider. They talk to me and listen to me, and together we have survived everything from earthquakes to budget cuts over the last few years. The whole Santa Cruz City-County Library System staff, from bottom to top, have been the people who have coped with change, dealt with problems, invented solutions on the spot, and taught me what I need to know so that I can give other people advice about handling problem situations.

Certain people played key roles in helping me revise this book. Attorney Mary Minow read and commented on the revision to Chapter 1 no less than four times. I am very grateful to her. Marcia Schneider of the San Francisco Public Library made extremely helpful comments on the revisions to Chapter 6 on censorship. And Gordon M. Conable, president of the Freedom to Read Foundation, took time from his very busy schedule to write a flattering new foreword, for which I thank him very much.

I would also like to thank the librarians, old friends and new, who read the manuscript or allowed themselves to be interviewed (formally and informally) for one or the other editions of this books. From California: Mary Franich Bignell (Santa Cruz) Rosie Brewer (Monterey), Gordon Conable (Riverside), Susan Fuller (Santa Clara), Nora Jacob (Santa Ana), Heidi Jaeger and Barbara Kiehl (both of Santa Cruz County), Wayne Mullin (Santa Cruz), Cathy Page (San Francisco), Ellen Pastore (Pacific Grove), and Beverley Simmons (Ventura). From Alachua County, Florida: Linda Luke, Adrian Mixon, and Meridith Pierce. Also, Judith Drescher (Memphis, Tennessee), Carole Hildebrande (Eugene, Oregon) Bonnie Isman (Amherst, Massachusetts), Mary Mahoney (Chelmsford, Massachusetts), Neel Parikh (University Place, Washington), Dallas Shaffer (Bainbridge Island, Washington), Nancy Milnor Smith (Galveston, Texas), Pat Woodrum (Tulsa, Oklahoma) and all the library workers who attended a Santiago Library System workshop on handling problem situations in October 1992.

John Barisone is the Santa Cruz City Attorney; all librarians should be so lucky as to have access to the kind of legal coaching he gives and to work with an attorney who reads books. Chris Hansen is a staff counsel at the American Civil Liberties Union in New York. He worked on the Child Internet Protection

Act case, and also took time to read and comment on my chapter about behavior rules.

Finally, I am very grateful for the comments on the first edition provided by my late father, management consultant Donald B. Tweedy, and my mother, editor Jessie M. Tweedy. Steve Turner, to whom I am married, is a professional writer. His editorial hand improves everything I write, and the intelligence of his insights into issues of library policy is invaluable.

Santa Cruz, California
May 2004

Part I
Writing Good Rules

Chapter 1

Making Behavior Rules

Does everyone remember the old "Twilight Zone" television show in which the narrator (Rod Serling) sets the scene? *Consider this ... a moment ... a moment when a man, an ordinary man, goes for a drive, and....* I'm reminded of that preparation when I look at the library's front steps on many mornings.

> *Consider this ... a building, a substantial building which houses books, where a woman, a once-attractive woman, now wearing a green raincoat and nothing else, waits to enter. And a man, a man carrying a bundled bedroll, also waits. A car drives up and a child climbs out. The car drives away. A person approaches the door of the building from the inside, unlocks it, holds it open. The people outside rush in.*

Who would have recognized this scene thirty years ago? Nobody but the staffs of public libraries in, say, downtown Los Angeles, New York, Boston, or St. Louis. Most people a la Norman Rockwell thought of libraries as cheerful and relatively sane places, to which citizens came to check out books, ask the odd question, and read the out-of-town newspapers. And they largely were.

But these days, the scene above is a familiar one in communities ranging from Farmington, New Mexico, to Amherst, Massachusetts. Society everywhere has changed. There are more visibly poor people, and more mentally disabled people on the street, and more children on their own, and many of them have nowhere to go for the day but the public library. There are also many more people endeavoring to manage lives complicated by inadequate childcare resources, or a job that has disappeared, or responsibility for elderly parents, and a thousand other social and economic problems.

So they come to the library, and the staff tries to meet whatever information needs they have, while at the same time coping with the special situations they create. The mess in the bathroom, made by a woman washing out her clothes. The anger of a well-dressed patron who is offended at the sight of the scruffy looking man in the torn jacket asleep in the magazine section. The Internet user who objects to the library's time rules. The woman who wants to check out a reference book, won't take no for an answer, and tells you so in a voice which can be heard upstairs in the children's room. The kids who think the disabled access ramp is the best place in town for skateboarding. The man who likes to follow around little girls. The guy who makes photocopies of fruit, usually citrus.

None of these people, and none of these situations, would surprise the vast majority of library workers today (although some would make them laugh). It is our working reality. Our task is to do our basic job—delivering information services to all the people—in the context of a world that is totally different than the one envisioned by those who first thought up the idea of public libraries.

As contemporary librarians we need to organize our rules for behavior, and train our staffs, so that we can cope effectively with this reality. This book is about doing that. It has four overriding themes.

The first is the most fundamental: *No one has the right to interfere with anyone else's right to use the library.* This is the premise upon which every behavior rule we make should be based. It is a simple one, and provided the rules we make to support it are equitably enforced, it is one we can stand on in any court of law.

The second theme is *that library staffs, and especially library managers, must be flexible in their approach to delivering information services in a rapidly changing world, and in devising the procedures and policies that organize how they do that.* A rule written for today may be totally inappropriate next week, next year, or even tomorrow. Being flexible means being willing to evaluate constantly, to throw out what is dearest to one's heart if it doesn't work, and (as a manager) to place a high value on the advice and judgement of the people who are serving the public on the front desk.

The third theme is that beyond certain minimum points, the more detailed we make our behavior rules, the more useless they are. The reason is that the people are *much* more creative than we are in thinking up things to do that we are not going to consider appropriate behavior in the library. Better to spend our time, and that of our staff, figuring out how to respond creatively to the unexpected. *Good procedures for handling bad situations are a whole lot more useful than good rules that don't prevent them.*

The final theme is that *people* are not the problem. The problem is the *situations* people create. *Our task is to learn how to handle problem situations, not problem people or problem patrons.*

It is true that we do need some rules. Among other reasons, the courts require it if we are going to impose legal sanctions on behavior that we do not regard as acceptable. We are also obligated legally to protect the staff and the property for which we are responsible.

The first part of this chapter is therefore about the legal and other bases that must be used in formulating these rules. [Appendices A and B include two documents of primary importance to discussions of these issues: the American Library Association *Library Bill of Rights*, and "Guidelines for the Development of Policies and Procedures Regarding User Behavior and Library Usage," written by ALA's Intellectual Freedom Committee.] The second part provides advice on the rule-setting process.

An important disclaimer must be emphasized. I am not an attorney, and I do not claim to be giving any librarian legal advice. My purpose is to sort out and put into readable language all the conflicting information that has been visited on us over the last several years. Three attorneys have reviewed and made suggestions about this chapter.[1] I believe it to be an accurate portrayal of the law as it is currently interpreted by the courts. But any library board and staff must rely on their own legal counsel for definitive advice.

Conduct and Free Speech: The U.S. Constitution

The courts distinguish between "rules governing pure conduct, which are merely subject to reasonableness (in relation to the library's purpose) and those that govern speech...."[2] Conduct rules are the ones about bringing coffee into the reading room or talking in a loud voice. Speech rules are about the information people have the right to access in the library and the library staff to select for the collections (obscene material? the Democratic Party Platform but not the Republican?). Although our focus in this chapter is behavior rules, we inevitably must discuss the legal underpinnings of access (speech) rules as well. The issue of access as it relates to the Internet is discussed in Chapter 7.

There are four basic sources underpinning behavior and access rules in libraries: the Constitution of the United States and other federal law, state constitutions, state and local laws, and local custom and culture. We begin with the U.S. Constitution, since it rightfully takes precedence over both state and local laws, and local custom.

> Congress shall make no law respecting an establishment of religion, or prohibiting the free exercise thereof; or abridging the freedom of speech, or of the press; or of the right of the people peaceably to assemble, and to petition the Government for redress of grievances.

This is the First Amendment to the Constitution, and the crucial phrase for our purposes is the one about "abridging the freedom of speech."

A key statement of the specific applicability to public libraries of the requirements of the First Amendment was in the 3rd Circuit Court of Appeals 1992 ruling in the case that is popularly called *Kreimer v. Morristown*.[3] In this case, the judges determined that the Morristown public library was a "limited" public forum.

The judges' opinion reviews a series of relevant Supreme Court cases, concluding that the First Amendment "does not merely prohibit the government from enacting laws that censor information, but additionally encompasses the positive right of public access to information and ideas."[4] While this right may not necessarily be unfettered, it does include the right to some level of access to a public library, "the quintessential locus of the receipt of information."[5]

This basic First Amendment principle is a fundamental guide for the development of behavior rules: *Part of any person's basic right to free speech is a right of access to information and ideas, including access to a public library.* And while the Library can adopt behavior rules, those rules will be scrutinized carefully by the courts to ensure that the First Amendment right is not abridged. If the rule is aimed at speech content the Court will impose *strict scrutiny.* If the rule is aimed at both speech and behavior, but not aimed at content, the Court will impose an *intermediate standard of scrutiny.* The Library must show that a significant library interest is served by the rule, that it is narrowly tailored to the purpose of the library, and that there are alternatives for securing information. A rule related to behavior and the library mission will be subject to a lower level of scrutiny known as a *reasonable or rational basis.*

Other important parts of constitutional law that affect both the behavior rules libraries make and how they are enforced are the guarantee of due process and equal protection contained in the Fourteenth Amendment. Although these concepts have changed over the years, basically due process means (according to Daniel Oran's *Law Directory for Non-Lawyers*) "that a person should always have notice and a real chance to present his or her side in a legal dispute...." The government (in this case, the states) cannot adopt laws that are arbitrary or unfair. And, the laws they adopt must provide definite standards for enforcement and provide a means for appeal.

In addition to his First Amendment claim, Richard Kreimer asserted he had been denied equal protection (and due process). He claimed that the behavior rules the library adopted denied him the same protection of the law enjoyed by other classes of persons. He was being treated unequally, he said, because he was homeless, and did not have access to the bathing facilities that the library's "personal hygiene" rules required. He also maintained that the Morristown library rules were vague. As noted, the Third Circuit Court of Appeals did not agree, but a lesson from the *Kreimer v. Morristown* case is that any library should be exceedingly careful in the way it defines its rules. Indeed, the Morristown Public Library amended several of its rules to make them more specific after the case was over.

In 2001 another homeless patron challenged the rules of the District of

Columbia Public Library on much the same grounds, and won. The rules in question contained provisions against "Conduct or personal condition objectionable to other persons using the Library's facilities…" and "Objectionable appearance (barefooted, bare-chested, body odor, filthy clothing, etc.)"[6]

The court ruled that the patron had been denied his First Amendment and Due Process rights. It used an intermediate standard of review, "narrowly tailored to the purpose of the institution." It found that the appearance regulation was vague and over broad, violating due process in that it failed to provide fair notice to its patrons or to meet constitutional standards prohibiting arbitrary enforcement of government regulations.[7]

In fact, a library that expects to enforce a specified odor regulation would be wise to develop some objective criteria for making its judgements. Bruce Ennis, Counsel for the Freedom to Read Foundation in the Kreimer v. Morristown case, has suggested possible objective tests, although he proposes them only as examples: Three other patrons must complain before a "smells bad" rule is invoked, or the library director and some number of patrons must agree that another patron smells intolerably bad.[8]

The subjectivity involved here is both dangerous and demeaning. Perhaps the American Library Association should commission high tech wizards to develop a "smell-o-meter" that could standardize our judgements. That way we could decide how to score someone who smells heavily of perfume or cologne, too. Some people are allergic to these sorts of fragrances; others are merely offended by them.

The smell-o-meter could come in two models. Model A would be for libraries with really big odor problems. It would attach to the front doors, and measure everyone who walked in. Presumably bells and whistles would go off when someone flunked.

Model B would be hand-held (say the size of a cell phone) and would be kept behind the circulation desk. When a patron complained about someone's body odor, special staff, probably dressed in white jump suits and boots, would quickly descend on the offensive person and measure him (or her), sort of like what the security guards in airports do.

In case you've missed it, I am joking about a very serious business because I think there are better ways to deal with smelly patrons than trying to enforce personal hygiene rules. We'll discuss the issue more in Chapter 2, which is about street people.

Local Laws and Ordinances

The great thing about local laws and ordinances, from the public library's perspective, is that there are so many of them. Over the years, our states and municipalities have managed to legislate practically everything that affects the security of a library building and its collections. This enables the library to post the law, cite the source (i.e., City of Worthy Ordinance Number 6792), and blame its putative unfairness on someone else. Look for rules about damaging property, harassing other people, and panhandling on public property in this category.

The bad thing about some local laws and ordinances is that they may not meet the U.S. Constitutional tests described in the previous section. For example, back in the 1950s many public libraries in the South had segregated reading rooms, restrooms, water fountains, and the like, mandated by local ordinance. The anti-gay ordinances of the 1990s may have had the same effect.

It is also true that many City Attorneys, County Counsels, and other governmental legal advisors, do not necessarily have special expertise in matters of information theory and law, free speech, or the special status of libraries as limited public forums. Their long experience in reviewing public works contracts may have left no time for thinking of the library in any terms but those of recreational reading.[9] The librarian's task has to be to educate these legal officers if possible, and if not to find alternative legal advice. The surest source of good advice will be the American Library Association's Office of Intellectual Freedom, or your state library association.

Local Custom and Culture

Legally, the most tenuous basis for making rules and regulations governing library use is "local custom." But this is the thin ice upon which many libraries' conduct codes are based. Sheltering with the majority yields a feeling of security, not to mention political protection. And indeed, this is a very comfortable position, right up to the moment when librarians and their trustees are hauled into court by a litigious rule violator who has read the First Amendment.

In its best application, local custom helps sort out rule-making issues into two categories: those that everyone can agree on right away, and those that are going to have to be carefully negotiated.

Presumably the first category would include prohibitions against smoking, damaging library materials, or eating and drinking in the main reading room. Viewing sexually explicit sites on the Internet (e.g., pornography) might fall in this category too. However, this is a very complicated issue that is discussed at greater length in Chapter 7.

In the second category are all the rules and potential rules which will fail the First and Fourteenth Amendment tests unless they are very carefully crafted indeed: the ones about loitering, or smelling bad, or sleeping, or harassing the staff.

"Local custom" may be the rubric attached by the Library Board, the City

Council, the Friends, or even the staff to their own definitions of appropriate behavior, but it is astonishing how frequently (and quickly) real disagreement emerges about what local custom actually is. Fortunately, these disagreements provide the opportunity for assessment of the library's situation, and its need for rules, in terms of larger legal requirements.

Writing Rules That Work

There probably isn't a librarian alive who doubts the premise that it is better to have planned ahead than to be stuck with no procedures at a moment of crisis. When you come upon a couple in a carrel near the 900s engaged in what can only be described as explicit sex, it is surely a thousand times better to know exactly what to do, than it is to stand there with an incredulous look on your face wondering why they didn't teach you about this in library school.

Making rules and policies in advance allows one to consider the situation, whatever it is, objectively, and outside the context of the particular perpetrators of the moment. As discussed above, this is very important in the context of the First Amendment. But even if that weren't the case, it makes for better policy.

Getting ready for both the predictable and the unpredictable gives the rule-writer the opportunity to step back and think, "What is the problem here? What change in the situation would fix it? Are we facing situations in which a *rule* is the answer, or would staff training in how to handle varieties of behavior be a better approach?"

The problem, for example, might be that a number of library users like to bring coffee and Danish from the take-out place on the corner into the main reading room. The resulting trash is attracting pests, and more than one cup of coffee has been knocked over onto reference materials or has stained the rugs.

The obvious solution is to make a rule that says no food or drink in the Library, although better phrasing might be "No Eating or Drinking," or "Eating and Drinking are Permitted in the Lobby Only." For the purists among your patrons, with the latter language you aren't forbidding people to have candy bars in their pockets.

Ah, but you are wondering how to write a rule forbidding carrel sex, and the answer is, you shouldn't even try. This is a true story, by the way—it happened at the Central Branch of the Santa Cruz Public Library. The staff person who handled it said to the participant he could see, "I don't think that is appropriate behavior in the library, do you?"

"No," she said, "I don't," and the couple desisted. If they hadn't stopped, he would have warned them, and eventually called the police, because lewd and lascivious behavior in public places is illegal in California.

The real question here is how often a library staff is actually confronted with that kind of behavior. The answer is rarely. And therefore, a rule forbidding it, particularly a posted one, does little more than make the library look silly. Think about it:

> WELCOME TO THE PEOPLE'S PUBLIC LIBRARY!
> No Smoking (City of Worthy Ordinance # 6793)
> Eating and Drinking are Permitted in the Lobby Only
> No Overt or Explicit Physical Sexual Behavior, Either Alone
>   or With A Partner

There are laws in nearly every state and local community that ban lewd behavior, carrying and displaying firearms in a manner that endangers the public, drinking alcohol or using drugs in public, and a variety of other behaviors that are inappropriate because they cause problems in a library. If a library is tormented by these kinds of behaviors on a regular basis, then the statement it ought to post is:

> The Library staff will apply all local ordinances and state laws that apply to behavior in public places as well as those regarding defacement of public property, and call the Police Department to help enforce them when necessary.

It is true, however, that there are certain rules a library may wish to post, even if local or state laws apply. A ban on smoking is a good example. Although these days smoking is prohibited in many public buildings, lots of people who smoke need to be reminded of that. Razor-blading out the pages from magazines constitutes abusing public property, and is also illegal in most jurisdictions. But the library might prefer to post a rule about damaging library property just to make sure there is no confusion.

A library might also wish to consider establishing a rule limiting use of certain library areas to patrons who are actually using the materials contained in that collection. The obvious example of this is the Children's Room, where the library can use such a rule to help itself create a safer environment for children. Chapter 4 on sexually deviant behaviors discusses this matter.

There is some disagreement among librarians and their supporters as to whether a library really needs to actually *post* its rules at all. The side opposed argues that provided a copy of the rules is available for scrutiny at a public desk, posting the rules is a negative image that only gives people bad ideas. They suggest that if a problem develops, giving a violating patron a clear oral warning, as well as a statement of the consequences of failing to comply with the rule, is all that is required.

Others believe that regardless of whether the law actually requires it, the rules we set for behavior must be posted so that there is no confusion as to what they are. One reason is that some signs, as for example those for No Smoking, are so ubiquitous that their *absence* authorizes the behavior. And as one librarian pointed out, "It may be true that after a while the posted rules become part of the furniture, and no one sees them, but I feel a lot more comfortable sending staff out to deal with problems if I know we did our best to inform people ahead of time of what we expect from them."

The specific rules the library decides it does need to post should be written in language which makes a clear statement of the unacceptable (or acceptable) behavior: "Please talk in soft tones only" is a better rule than "Quiet Please." "Children under 9 must be supervised by a person 14 years of age or older" is a very specific statement that covers two problems at once: young children left alone at the library, and young children in the care of young siblings.

Common sense suggests that the consequences of not following the rules should also be stated clearly. Probably this is best done at the top of the posted rules:

> If you fail to follow the Library's behavior rules, the staff may require you to leave. Damaging or destroying library materials, equipment, or furniture can result in suspension of your library borrowing privileges, as well as criminal prosecution.

One problem in writing good rules is balancing the needs of the larger group (either patrons or staff) with those of individual users, especially in the context of First Amendment rights. By the same token, a library needs to protect the rights of the larger group too. No one denies, for example, that people with physical disabilities have the same rights of access to information as those without. But, e.g., does a hearing impaired user over in the Periodicals Area have the right to shout comments on the news of the day to his companion? And the companion to shout back?

It may be that the balanced approach will have to be achieved in the *enforcement*, rather than in the rule itself. The staff, for instance, may tolerate the hard-of-hearing person's voice level when he or she is asking for information or help, but insist on reasonable quiet when the conversation is merely social.

There is one final test to apply to all the rules the library makes. It is standing back, looking at the rule, and asking, "Is it possible to misconstrue this rule? Is there any way anyone could use this rule to discriminate against someone else?" If the answer is yes, start again. And when you do that, start by asking (again) what problem the rule is intended to solve. Is a rule a good method for mitigating the problem situation, or would better enforcement techniques by the staff help more?

Caution: Any rule that has anything to do with physical appearance probably falls in this category. Even a rule which says a patron must wear a shirt and shoes offers room to quibble over the definition of shoes (are sandals shoes?), as well as what "wearing" really means, not to mention the definition of a shirt. Does "wearing" include a shirt hung over naked shoulders? Maybe in the eyes of a tired circulation desk worker, invoking the rule will depend on whether the shirtless person is tanned and clean shaven, or bearded and dirty.

With all of the above in mind, here's a checklist for evaluating library behavior rules as they are conceptualized and written:

1. *Does the problem behavior interfere with anyone else's right to use the library?* If it doesn't, don't bother to make a rule about it.

2. *Is the problem behavior already covered by local ordinance or state law?* If so, is there a good reason why the library needs to restate it?

3. *Is a rule an appropriate means for substantially mitigating a situation caused by the problem behavior?* If it isn't, find another way to address the problem. These could range from special staff training to cooperative approaches with other community agencies.

4. *Does the rule address a situation created by problem behavior, or is the rule really aimed at a specific individual or a group of people?* If it is, find another way to deal with him/her/them.

5. *Does a rule forbidding this behavior meet First Amendment tests?* Is it narrowly tailored to the purpose of the library and does it protect a significant government interest? Does it leave open an alternative channel for receiving information and ideas?

6. *Can the majority of people understand the wording used to write this rule?* This is not an issue of whether the library's rules should be posted in languages other than English: Of course they should be if the library has significant user groups who have English as a second language. The issue is deciding whether most of the library's patrons will understand phrases such as "failure to mitigate the loud and obnoxious behavior will result in immediate..."

7. *Can the majority of people understand what will happen if they don't follow the rule?*

8. *Is the rule clear enough so that there is no possibility that a member of the staff can misconstrue it?*

9. And a year later, *do we still need this rule, and does it continue to meet the first eight criteria?*

If all your rules can survive this examination, then get them printed and posted.

Part II

Problems That Plague Us

Chapter 2

Street People,
the Mentally Disabled,
Substance Abusers, and
Other Symbols of Our Times

Let's face it. The boring majority of library problems are caused by everyday patrons who are angry and take it out on the library staff. Indeed, these often take consummate skill and patience to defuse. But they seem so normal: The "glamour" problems of the 1990s and early 21st century—situations involving street people, mentally disabled people, substance abusers, and the like—are what most library workers want to know how to handle. So let's start with these, and come back to angry people in Chapter 3.

There are two issues here. The first is how library staff should handle the specific problem situations that street people—including the mentally disabled and substance abusers—create. Never mind, for the moment, about potential limitations on their right to be in the library, and what the larger community response to the problem should be. The reality is they *are* in the library, and their behavior can create problems for staff and for other users. How should these be handled?

The second issue is how public libraries should cope with the fact that as poverty and other social ills increase in this country, the number of people on the streets with nowhere else to go (and therefore hanging around libraries) is also increasing. Are public libraries being turned into dumping grounds for society's problems? If they are, what can we do about it?

First, some definitions. *"Street people"* is the term I am going to use in discussing the raunchy looking folks, usually men but women too, who tend to travel with most of their worldly possessions in trash bags or bedrolls, wear very ragged clothes, often haven't bathed lately, and may or may not exhibit various eccentric or anti-social behaviors indicative of mental illness, alcoholism, or other substance abuse. The defining characteristic of the street person in this chapter is *appearance*.

In other times street people were called "vagrants," a term that has legal weight but is no longer much in fashion. "Bum," "beggar," and "hobo" have also been used. In some river towns street people are called "trolls" because they often camp under bridges. "Transient" comes closest in some ways to describing the population that worries library staffs and users, but that description still is not sufficient.

Homeless people are not necessarily street people, which is why I am not using that more common term. In fact, the majority of homeless persons in the nation are single mothers and their dependent children. And these days there also are plenty of neatly dressed men and women with jobs who have no place to live. They are not the ones who are causing problems for public libraries. Nor are all alcoholics or mentally disabled persons street people. We all know about alcoholics who apparently lead normal lives, and people with serious mental illness who are not living on the street (but some of whom come in and create library problems anyway).

What problem a street person causes depends on what rules for behavior a library has adopted. A street person is not a problem simply because of his or her appearance or putative life style. It is what the street person *does* in the library that may or may not create a problem for the library staff.

A *"mentally disabled"* person is defined here as someone who, regardless of appearance, acts out in a dysfunctional way, creating a disturbance which breaks a rule or otherwise interferes with someone else's right to use the library. For example, a midwestern public library has a patron we'll call Mrs. Wallace. She is a neatly dressed woman in her late forties who likes to read mysteries. A frequent library visitor, she conducts conversations across the library table with her companion, whom we'll call Mrs. Righter, often in a loud voice.

The problem is that Mrs. Righter does not exist, except of course in the mind of Mrs. Wallace. Mrs. Wallace is mentally disabled. We'll come back to this situation to learn how a clever library staff member solved the problem this non-threatening but disruptive person was creating.

A *"substance abuser"* is anyone who is wigged out on alcohol, drugs, or whatever, and is causing a problem for other library users because of it. Lots of people abuse substances without preventing someone else from using the library: Eating too much or smoking heavily come immediately to mind. I am emphasizing this simple-minded point only to remind us that we are focusing on problem behaviors here, not generic categories of people.

Coping Techniques and a Lengthy Example

Since the *Kreimer v. Morristown* case, I've heard many library workers, when discussing problem situations with street people or the mentally ill, say "I didn't want to violate his rights. I was afraid if I did the wrong thing I'd get the library in trouble—that he'd sue us or something."

We need to get to the common ground. We don't want to violate users' rights. We don't want them to violate our rights or the rights of other users. It is the responsibility of library management to ensure that the library has rules for behavior that meet constitutional requirements, and that staff is trained to enforce them equitably and sensibly. If management has done its job, no library worker should have to worry that she or he is violating someone's rights.

I suggest four tools to help a library staff cope with the problems created by street people, mentally disabled people, and substance abusers in libraries. The first three can be taught with staff training: *knowing the library's rules and how to enforce them, remembering to consult one's colleagues, and using teamwork to deal with specific problems.*

The fourth tool is common sense, an attribute that rarely appears in a job description, but is crucial for most library workers. It may be a genetic trait, but common sense definitely can be improved via experience and training.

Here's a lengthy example. I use it because it illustrates the worst of all possible scenarios: a tiny branch potentially dominated by the problems created by a mentally disabled person.

The Santa Cruz City County Library System was recently host to a mentally ill, quasi-street person patron (he was an off-again, on-again resident of halfway houses) I'll call Gene. Gene had visited several branches, everywhere creating problems, ranging from obnoxious body odor through shouting, to potential sexual harassment of staff. His choice of branch location depended on where he was living at the moment.

Gene was physically imposing: 6'4", 230 pounds, beard, dreadlocks, and a big, deep voice. His behaviors seemed to be motivated by desire for attention. He talked loudly to himself and imaginary people, making repetitive statements such as "I am a powerful Black man." He mumbled and grunted. Periodically he asked help at the reference desk in finding materials, but his requests were repetitive. He remembered certain people, such as a branch manager, but he did not have any long-term memory for rules or consequences. For this reason, it did not do any good to ban him from the library for three days as a "lesson" or punishment, because on the fourth day he'd be back with the same behavior.

Accosting women was one of Gene's typical behaviors, especially if the woman was African American. He also sometimes tried to touch young children, particularly African American children and those who were on their own, although this did not seem to be sexual behavior so much as simply finding human contact.

Gene's modus operandi was to come into the branch and establish himself in a reference area chair for the day. There would be no particular problem with this, except that his recent branch of choice was very small (only one large room). Since Gene rarely bathed or changed his clothes, his sometimes-nauseating body odor dominated the branch. He also wanted to be in physical contact with the branch's page (an African American college student). He'd follow her about from book stack to book stack, trying to stand close to her.

And Gene was a shouter. Asked to leave, or to go outside for awhile, he would stand on the entrance steps and complain about life in general and the status of Black men in society. None of his comments made much sense, but his stage-like presence by the door did have a chilling effect on people visiting this small town branch.

Barbara Kiehl, our branch manger, hit easily on one of the tools needed for handling this kind of situation: "The other branch managers clued me in," she says. "He isn't dangerous, but you do have to be completely straightforward. If I wanted Gene to be quieter I had to say so, and tell him what would happen if he wasn't. In the first days, I guess I let myself be intimidated by him, and spent too much time just putting up with him."

Barbara also told me that after she noticed Gene looking over the younger children at the branch, she took the branch's three frequent latchkey girls aside and encouraged them to be sure to tell her if anyone they didn't know tried to touch them. A few days later one of the children indeed reported that Gene had tried to sit too close to her, and that she had told him to go away. Barbara immediately told Gene to cease and desist, and warned him she would call the sheriff if he touched a child again. He stopped that behavior.

The problem with the page required implementing the advice we have received from trainers who are expert in teaching women to defend themselves: Make the unacceptable behavior clear to the person doing it, set limits, and stick to them. The page had to steel herself to say to Gene, "No, I do not *want* you to stand there. You are standing too close to me. You are preventing me from doing my work. Please stop it."

This clear statement enabled her supervisor to deal directly with violations of the limits set, escalating eventually to a call to law enforcement if this was necessary.

When Gene smelled so bad that in the opinion of the branch manager he was interfering with other peoples' right to use the library, she asked him to leave. She told him he could come back when he had washed himself and his clothes. She knew he had the means to do this, because at the time he was living in a nearby group home. And yes, this was a judgment call.

Did she use some version of the smell-o-meter? No, even California doesn't have that technology yet. Did she get three patrons to agree? No, the Santa Cruz Library System hasn't made a behavior rule which requires complaints from a specified number of other patrons in a small branch before the branch manager can politely ask a person to leave (see Chapter 1). We rely on the common sense and judgment of the branch manager who is on the site. One reason is that we know what smells bad at a branch the size of Barbara's wouldn't be noticed at the much larger downtown facility.

We expect the branch manager to evaluate the situation. Has anyone complained? Are people moving away from the area where he is? Are you yourself made sick by the odor? If any of these apply, ask another staff person to smell the area. If you both think the odor is interfering with other peoples' rights, tell the offender to leave until he has cleaned himself and his clothes.

Gene's talking and shouting behavior on the front steps of the library presented a special problem because it occurred outside the library, potentially locating him in the territory of a traditional public forum. On the other hand, nobody is allowed to block the entrance of a public building, and the entrance steps are narrow. With a more litigious-minded person, this might not have worked, but Barbara solved it by telling him, "This behavior is inappropriate. If you don't stop right now and move on, I will call the sheriff." And in court the library would certainly have argued that Gene was stopping other people from using the branch.

Barbara also reported that she called the group home where Gene lived to talk with the supervisor about persuading him to bathe more frequently. She didn't get very far: "No, I can't do anything about that" and "No there is nothing I can do" was the unhelpful response. We'll return to this supervisor in the second part of this chapter.

In the meantime, the story of Gene and the small branch ended with the news that he was required to move out of his group home, and stopped coming to that library. So this particular mentally disabled/street person problem for our small branch evaporated when Gene moved away (although he was spotted at the downtown branch a few weeks later, meaning that the Library probably hasn't seen the last of Gene and the problems he creates). But suppose that coincidental solution hadn't happened? What would the branch manager have done next? It seems to me there were two options.

The first was to continue to endure, taking the same decisive approach: when Gene's talk was too loud, telling him he had be quiet or to leave. If his body odor was too great, telling him to go and clean up—the library worker's directive in this case apparently carrying more weight than that of the group home supervisor. If he touched a child or harassed a page, the same applied, with escalation to law enforcement if necessary.

The alternative in dealing with a situation like this is to create a case file that can be used to secure a court order preventing the person from coming into the library. As Director of Libraries I would have had no objection to doing this in Gene's case. He was abusing a tiny branch by seriously interfering with its intended purpose as a public library and with the rights of other people to use its resources. The judgment might well be different at a larger facility, where staff and patrons have many more options for seating and so forth.

Getting a court order against a patron is a strategy that needs the cooperation of the library's legal counsel and local law enforcement officials. Meeting with them *before* there is a case in hand, and agreeing on how this strategy might work, is absolutely crucial. They will tell the library staff what documentation is needed, and it is up to the library to create staff procedures that ensure that the data is there when push comes to shove.

The usual case file includes a complete log by the branch manager of every encounter with the patron, what both the staff and the patron did or said, and what the outcome was. Verification by other staff (the page, the library clerk) would be required. Also needed, but hardest to obtain, would be supporting statements by other patrons.

It is a sad comment on our times that people are willing to complain about problem situations, but are so frequently *unwilling* to take personal and "official" responsibility for what they don't like. A staff person says, "I'm writing down what you say. Will you sign it please, so that we can use it if we have to call the police?" And the patron says, "Oh, no. I can't get involved in anything like that." This is the same person who thinks "they"—meaning us—should do something about such-and-such a problem.

My own conviction is that a direct statement to a complaining patron is the best strategy. If someone objects to someone else's behavior, and then says she or he won't put her name on the dotted line, tell her/him that the library cannot find permanent solutions to bad behavior by an habitual offender if other patrons aren't willing to make official complaints. At least try to extract the patron's name and phone number for the file, so that if the library does end up requesting a court order, he or she can be tracked down for a statement.

And I hope no one has missed the obvious point that good record keeping is crucial. Any library should have a standard form on which the staff can report incidents of one sort or another. Ongoing situations, such as the ones created by Gene, should be logged by the branch manager, who may end up finding that keeping a Gene Diary (or whatever) is satisfyingly therapeutic.

Handling Gene involved knowing the library rules and how to enforce them, consultation with other library staff, and a strong dose of the branch manager's common sense. I want to add a few more words on the latter trait.

Part of common sense, it seems to me, is accepting people, even mentally disabled people, for who and what they are, and dealing with them on their own terms. One of my favorite examples of this is a story told by Julia Orozco, the Director of the Steinbeck Library in Salinas, California. A patron was *bang-*

ing, banging, banging on the keyboard of one of the public access catalog terminals. A staff person asked him to stop, and he said, "I can't. I'm telecommunicating with the spirits."

The staff person looked at him and said, "This is the *wrong terminal* for that," and she managed to ease him out the door.

Further east, in the Memphis–Shelby County Library System, one of the branches had a patron who liked to copy pieces of fruit on the copy machine. Every couple of weeks he'd come in and spend time making photocopies of real sliced oranges or grapefruit. Naturally enough, the staff was not particularly pleased by this behavior, although the library doesn't have a posted rule saying "No Copying of Fruit." The copier glass had to be cleaned every time he came in, so one day a staff person approached him and said,

"Mr. Jameson, I *understand* that you need to copy fruit. *We* need you to clean up the copy machine afterwards."

"Oh," said Mr. Jameson. "Okay."

And the next time he came in, he copied fruit as usual, and then took a paper out of his pocket and wiped down the copy machine. End of problem.

Remember Mrs. Wallace, who talked too loudly to her imaginary friend, Mrs. Righter? Once, when a staff person approached Mrs. Wallace and asked her to lower her voice, she said, "I can't. Mrs. Righter keeps asking me questions and she's hard of hearing, you know."

"Oh," said the staff person. "All right. Mrs. Righter, will you please be quiet now?" And Mrs. Righter was, and so was Mrs. Wallace for the rest of that day.

Teamwork in handling problem situations is crucial, and the term means more than simply two people approaching a scary patron, or one staff person backing up another in a difficult encounter. It is also collectively developing responses to difficult situations by consulting and comparing notes.

A year of so ago the Santa Cruz library system had a nine-year-old kid who specialized in being super-demanding. He was very bright and seductively curious, but there was no satisfying him. He wouldn't let go once a staff person started helping him. Robert, we'll call him, would ask question after question, obsessing on a subject. And he'd repeat and repeat the same question, moving from one public desk to another, insisting on far more help than any individual can reasonably demand in a very busy library. He'd come back, too, the next day, with the same question, or another, and start again.

Staff conversation established that the child who had become a problem at all desks at Central and at his neighborhood branch was, indeed, the same Robert. The collective, creative response was to devise a ticket system for the child that would limit his access to staff help.

The staff didn't feel right about limiting service to a child without explaining to the parent, so they phoned Robert's mother. Surprise! She told them that Robert is a "high functioning autistic" child, versus the hyperactive diagnosis we had made. Coming to the library is part of his entry into the world, his mother said. He is learning how to handle real world situations, which is why she comes in with him, but only sits and reads magazines, and doesn't intervene in his interactions with the staff. (We all knew we signed on as psychotherapists, right?)

The real world experience we devised for Robert was to make tickets for him in the Children's Room at the Central Branch. His neighborhood Branch Manager does the same thing. Each ticket entitles him to one question or one subject. When a ticket is used up, the staff person involved says, "I've helped you all that I can." He watches while the staff person puts a big check on the slip, and then throws it away, physically emphasizing that the question is done. When he has used up all his tickets for the day, the staff person says, "I've helped you all that I can. Now you need to find something else to do." The precise language in each case is part of the programmed response.

I am aware that anyone reading this story who works in a big city library will believe that only a small town operation could afford to put this kind of attention into finding a "fix" for the problems created by one small patron. I'm not so sure that's true, for the simple reason that Robert was driving everyone crazy. It was easier for the staff to get together and figure something out, than to leave the solution to chance. Wouldn't that be true in a big library too?

One thing about the Robert case that aggravates me, however, is the expectations of Robert's mother. The library staff are neither social workers nor special education teachers. She nevertheless assumed that because we were there and available, we'd be able provide the "real world" experiences her son needs. She had no thought for how difficult our staff might find the child's tormenting behavior, nor that the staff had obligations to other patrons that might be sacrificed to meet Robert's needs.

The tempering factor in creative responses of this sort is available staff time and energy. I can imagine situations in which Robert might have to be limited to one question per day, for instance. But it is hoped that the instinctive response—"Get this kid out of my hair"—will not be allowed to overwhelm the prudent operational compassion which should be a hallmark of library dealings with the mentally afflicted.

Appendix C, the Santa Cruz problem situation manual, also contains interleaved sample procedures from other libraries for handling street people, mentally disabled people, and substance abusers. These samples have one particularly important common theme not yet mentioned: If a staff person has any reason to believe that a patron—especially a substance abuser—is dangerous, call the police. If you are at a geographically isolated facility, get backup from someone else—the sheriff, the fire department, someone—before you approach the patron.

Symbols of Our Times

In his fascinating 1992 book, *The Visible Poor—Homelessness in the United States,*[1] Joel Blau makes the point that people get angry with street people and beggars (the "homeless" in common parlance) because it is very hard to avoid actually *seeing* them. Other kinds of poverty endemic in our society—single mothers on welfare, migrant farm workers living in camps with no toilets, elderly people alone in single room occupancy hotels—can all be avoided by the simple means of organizing one's life correctly. It is much harder to miss the sight of a "derelict" sitting on the Main Street sidewalk, or a street person reading the newspaper at the public library.

The first response of far too many people to the sight of poverty is anger at the victim. And when the victims use the community institutions, such as libraries, which people regard as their own (even if they don't want to spend a lot of tax money supporting them), they get even madder. They generalize and stereotype, labeling anyone who fails to meet their standards of dress and hygiene as a "street person homeless bum." They transfer anger to the library staff for "putting up with those people." And they dramatize their lack of comfort with the unknown by expressing fears for their personal safety.

The irony of the situation, of course, is that many of these same complaining people are not willing to address the systemic economic and social problems that have created the "visible poor" in the first place. This leaves public libraries and their staffs in the wretched position of needing to honor the First Amendment rights of everyone to use their facilities, at the same time that their traditional support constituencies back out the door in disgust at who is also using the library.

I don't have a solution to this problem, but I do think libraries can take a two-pronged approach to finding one. The first approach involves education of their traditional users and supporters, and the second is community organization for change. And I have an observation to share about the changes that (surprisingly) Internet access has made in our perception of street people in the library.

Standing up for the First Amendment right of all people to have access to the information the library provides is an obligation of all public library workers, both because it is the law, and because it is right. First we must adopt behavior rules that ensure that no one interferes with anyone else's right to use the library. And we must train our staffs in how to enforce those rules equitably. Then we must be willing to say to our library board members, donors, regular mystery readers, politicians, and anyone else who asks, "We do not make aesthetic judgments about who can use the library. *You* have to tell *me* how that person whose looks or smell you don't like is interfering with your library use." It is not easy, but if you say it often enough, people eventually begin to understand.

The public library staff is also entitled to say to its community, its governing authorities, and its newspapers, "Wait a minute. We are the public library, and we have a very difficult and complex job to do meeting the information needs of all the people. You must confront, whether you like it or not, the fact that there are a lot of poor people in this community who have nowhere to go all day. They come to the library, which is their right, but providing day center service is not our job. What can we do about this?"

That is basically what Pat Woodrum, Director of the Tulsa (Oklahoma) Public Library, did some years ago, when a large population of homeless people was occupying the library's main facility. After one false start, she managed to get the Community Service Council, churches, members of the Library Commission, and other groups to work together to find a solution to the problem—a Day Center at which the library had a literacy program and a deposit collection and other services are provided.[2] And the solution has held. In mid–2003 the Day Center is still in business, offering counseling services, limited help, and referrals, especially to the families and children caught in bad situations. The Tulsa library provides the Day Center with books, magazines and other materials from its endless stream of gift materials.

Woodrum used persistence, and her library's long tradition of cooperation with other community groups to deal with this problem. I also suspect that she was ultimately successful because she was willing to be direct in her statement of the need, to say to the people of Tulsa, "We have a problem here. What are *we* going to do about it."

Here's the observation, which comes from Richard Parker, in 2003 the Deputy Director of the Tulsa City County Library. Ten years ago homeless people seemed to be loafing at the library, staring forlornly at other customers or staff. These days they are using the public access computers, and are therefore more accepted as regular library customers. The computers seem to have moved everyone, including street people, into the visual main stream.[3]

Remember the Santa Cruz branch manager who got the run-around from the group home supervisor, when she called to see if he could do something to get Gene to bathe more frequently? In retrospect, I am sorry we didn't call the county mental health department, and raise a tremendous stink (you should excuse it) about that response. The group home was operating under a profit-making contract from the county. The supervisor's *job* was to care for the people who lived in his facility, and he should have been *grateful* that a worker from another agency was trying to reach out to help one of his clients. Instead he shined us on, because he thought he could get away with it. We should have demanded action, and if we didn't get it, should have reported him to his funding authorities.

It is important to remember that there is a difference between being "abrasive," which heaven knows no librarian wants to be, and being willing to say out loud and directly what the problem is. My conviction is that librarians need to improve their skills in this. We need to say loudly that we are in the information business, not the shelter business, and that if shelter is the need, the community is going to have to find a way to meet it. We will help, but we will not do the whole job.

Ten Minutes a Week for Training

Every library does its best to train new workers in standard policies and procedures, usually after going through a hiring process which attempts to weed out the people whose communication skills are not strong enough to make it on the public desks. And most libraries try to send staff to occasional training workshops on special subjects.

However, what with budget crises, and automation system upgrades, and constantly increasing demands for services, it is very easy for even the best of libraries to fall down in its program of ongoing training. Avoid this if you possibly can; training and retraining for all staff is immensely important. It helps them stay fresh, it reminds workers of what library policy is, and it provides therapy for people who are working in relatively stressful situations.

Another important reason why a library should find a way to make sure that ongoing training gets done is the window it provides supervisors on what is really going on in any library operation. Staff talk when they get together, and they tend to talk turkey if they are sharing information about problems. Listening to them is a great way to pick up on trouble situations before they get out of control.

One idea for institutionalizing a library's ongoing training program is to allocate ten or fifteen minutes out of every staff meeting for some sort of problem situation exercise. These can be the meetings each library department holds (the monthly meeting of the youth services staff, the biweekly circulation staff meeting, etc.) or the whole staff meeting at a branch. The point is to spend a little time, frequently, practicing and discussing how the staff handles problem situations. If you make role-playing assignments (when appropriate) and do the training exercise at the *beginning* of the meeting, you'll cut down on late arrivals (no one likes to miss the entertainment) and make sure you actually get the training done.

Here are four discussion questions related to handling problem situations created by mentally disabled people, substance abusers, and street people. There are no right answers—how a staff should respond to each problem depends upon the library's own procedures.

1. A page trying to shelve books runs her book truck into a backpack that has been left in the aisle. Just as she is moving it out of the way, a man who

smells like a brewery comes up and says, "Listen bitch. Don't you touch my stuff." What should the page do?

2. A patron comes to desk to complain about a dirty-looking person sitting in reading room. How does the staff person respond?

3. The director has had a call from the chair of the library board, who wants to know whether the library gives borrower cards to homeless people. The chair thinks the board ought to adopt a policy on that, and wonders what the staff would recommend.

4. A teacher turns up one morning with a group of eight obviously mentally retarded adults. The teacher doesn't ask for special help from the library staff, but other patrons are clearly very disturbed by the group. One of them finally complains. What should the staff do or say?

Chapter 3

Dealing with Angry People

At a training session for library workers in Southern California, the first half-hour was spent on a warm-up exercise that turned out to be fun for everyone. The group was asked to list the problems they had with library users that drove them the craziest. Probably about 60 percent of the workshop participants were circulation desk clerks and other public service support staff, so they really knew what goes on in libraries. Drunk and disorderly patrons, smelly street people, latchkey children, and sexual deviants were all mentioned.

But the overwhelming majority of the problems cited were those created by people who are angry at the library: mad because of an overdue notice they think was an error, mad because an item requested two days ago still isn't in, mad because they had trouble finding a parking space, mad because they couldn't find the deeply desired book on the shelves, mad because the library is closing at 9 P.M., mad because … you name it, a patron has gotten mad about it.

Judith Drescher, the Director of the Memphis–Shelby County Public Library and Information Center in Tennessee, suggests that the reason people get mad at the library is because their expectations are so high. They don't expect much from the Post Office or the Department of Motor Vehicles or even a department store. They expect to have to stand on line forever at government agencies, and to obey rules such as needing your credit card if you want to charge something.

But libraries are supposed to be different. They are pleasant places, with comfortable chairs, and they have books and magazines, and even videos and records. And the staff, who are often one's friends, or the daughter of one's neighbor, are nice too. They smile, and help you find things.

So when the library enforces a rule, such as needing your card to check something out, or dares to send you a notice about a book you know you returned last week, or fails to get you something you really want to read right now, WELL!!! It is unexpected, unreasonable, wrong, and well worth getting mad about. What is the world coming to, after all, when even the library starts sending those awful computer printed notices one can hardly read, and can't even keep bestsellers on the shelves? And so forth.

This chapter is about helping staff deal with people who are mad. "Active listening," coupled with reasonable assertiveness and a few tricks collected from libraries around the country, are the basis of the coping techniques described.

There is a lot of literature on personal communication skills. One of the most interesting is Sandra A. Crowe's *Since Strangling Is Not an Option,*[1] which aside from a great title, offers tricks and advice based on a lot of concrete examples. There are also quite a few psychologists, social workers, and academics who run sidelines in communications training, so it shouldn't be hard to find an expert to do a staff workshop if your library (or better, your library consortium) can afford it.

Basically, I want to make two points. The first is that every staff person at every level, from book shelvers to the director, needs to have good communications skills to handle the problems they'll confront in the library world. For those on the service desks, these skills include knowing how to keep cool and keep smiling when an angry patron is making every effort to provoke the opposite response.

The second is that sometimes even patrons are right: If an anger-making situation keeps coming up, probably the staff should take a look at the problem causing it, rather than worrying about whether or not the angry people are wrong to be mad.

Communications Skills

I once heard a police officer who specializes in community relations say that he is astounded at how little time the typical police academy puts into training cops to communicate well. "We don't just hand them a gun and say 'point it and fire it' do we? No, we put them through days, even weeks of firing practice, and they have to re-qualify every year. But we don't do anything like that with communications skills, and they use those more than they do their guns, or they ought to, anyway." He saw effective communication skills, and the need for training to acquire them, as one of the similarities between cops and library workers. The essence of effective communication, he thought, was translating what people *said* into what they really *meant*.

This is also a part of "active listening," the technique Thomas Gordon popularized by turning it into Parent Effectiveness Training. The active listening idea is to acknowledge (or accept) the other person's feelings, so that the two of you can get on with finding out what the real problem is. It also uses the "I-messages" and "You-messages" of assertiveness to establish ownership of ideas and emotions, and defuse tense situations.

Here's an example of active listening from an article Nathan M. Smith and Irene Adams wrote for the periodical *Public Libraries:*[2]

USER: Boy, what a crummy library! Who organized this place anyway? This is the biggest mess I've ever seen!

STAFF: (Using non-active listening) Yes, it could be better organized, but that's only one opinion. We do our best to make it work. If you really have a complaint, take it to the director's office.

The trouble with this response, Smith and Adams point out, is that it is defensive, and doesn't recognize that the patron is simply taking his frustration out on the librarian. A better, active listening response, would be:

STAFF: It sounds like you've had a frustrating experience. Is there any way I can help you find what you need?

Frankly, I've always been faintly embarrassed by active listening examples. Reading them on the page, I usually feel about as comfortable with them as I did telling my adolescent son, "It makes me feel very annoyed when you don't clean your room." What, after all, could be more asinine than saying to a person with steam coming out of her ears, "You seem to be very upset." That kind of remark feels (you should excuse it) to me like an invitation for a punch in the nose, as in, "You *bet* I am, cookie, and you better just watch it."

However, I must confess that active listening has gotten many a teenager's room cleaned up, and often works to defuse the ire of people in unreasonable moods. The major problem is remembering to use it. It could be that this is harder for library directors than it is for desk staff who, after all, get much more day-to-day practice handling difficult people. In either case, practice helps, so be sure to read the last part of the chapter, which gives some advice about training sessions.

Of course, active listening isn't *always* an appropriate response. There's the anecdote—which I hope is fanciful—about the library worker who first practiced this newly-learned technique when an anguished patron rushed up to the circulation desk, asking, "Where's the men's room?"

"It sounds like you really *need* the men's room," responded the clerk, giving him a direct and sympathetic gaze and then maintaining a slow, careful demeanor as she fetched him the key.

The balance of the tale involves some mess on the way to the restroom—an outcome that surely added to the day's list of angry user complaints—not to mention some resentment from the custodian crew.

Since active listening is a "first step in the process" technique, what comes *after* it is important too. Communications specialists suggest that only 10 percent of everything we say is content. Another 30 percent is body language (eye contact, relaxed posture, etc.), and the balance the tone of voice. To demonstrate the latter, try saying this sentence aloud putting the emphasis on a different word each time:

I didn't say you stole the book.

I *didn't* say you stole the book.

I didn't *say* you stole the book.

I didn't say *you* stole the book.

I didn't say you *stole* the book.

I didn't say you stole the *book.*

What we are after in good communication is a perfect match between what we are saying, how we say it, and what our body is demonstrating we feel.

The Paraphrasing Technique

One technique that incorporates the principles of active listening and works well in getting through an angry encounter, is to paraphrase what the patron is saying, and try to make the patron paraphrase you right back. Here's an example of how it works. The scene involves a patron who is angry about the time limit for using an Internet terminal.

PATRON: I think it's outrageous that you are limiting my time at this terminal. I have as much right to use it as anybody else.

STAFF: You don't like our one-hour time limit for Internet use, is that what you're saying?

PATRON: Yes, that's right. And I don't understand why. I'm not done.

STAFF: Well, we have a one-hour limit on use of the Internet terminals so that as many people as possible can use them. We only have six here at this Branch and a lot of people need them. So we limit the time any one person can use them.

PATRON: But there isn't anybody waiting to use this terminal, so I shouldn't have to get off.

STAFF: You think you should be able to keep on using a terminal until somebody else wants it, right?

PATRON: Right. It's just going to stand here empty.

STAFF: We have our rule so that when someone comes in they see that a terminal is empty and they sign up to use it. If all the terminals are in use all the time people won't ask. So do you understand why we have the rule?

PATRON: I suppose so. But I still don't agree with it.

When people are very upset, they tend not to listen to each other. Instead, they spend the time the other person is talking thinking up what they will say next. Paraphrasing forces both people to listen, so that they can restate the other's position. Thus it is especially useful when the conflict is a very emotional. Paraphrasing does, of course, require a "contract" between the partners, and that is not always easy to achieve. At a minimum, though, a staff person can repeat back what the patron has said, and make slow progress towards getting the library's point across.

The "I Believe You" Technique

This technique could be used, for example, by the staff to handle patrons who claim that they already have returned an item for which they have received an overdue notice.

PATRON: I got this notice, and it really makes me so annoyed. I *know* I returned this book, and this is the second notice I've gotten for it.

STAFF: I believe you. Tell you what ... here's what we can do. Give me your card, and let's get your record up on the screen. [wands in borrower card, turns circulation terminal so that patron can see the record too]. Now, here's the item listed as overdue. I am going to mark it "Claims Returned," because that is what the computer calls it when we show the item as still out, but you say you returned it. *We'll* look for the item here and at the other branches, and I hope *you'll* look around at home too. Have you tried under the front seat of the car? I'm not joking—if we had a dollar for every time someone finds a book there, the library would have a much bigger budget ... okay??

PATRON: Well, is the book going to stay on my record forever?

STAFF: Not if we can find it. Or maybe *you'll* find it. Why don't you check back in a few weeks and see if it has turned up.

It is the policy of some libraries to clear most patron records, although they do keep track of how many "claims returned" items a patron has reported over the years. But whether patrons are forgiven for items that never turn up is not the point. What's important here is the basic positive style of the staff response to the patron.

The Stand and Deliver Technique

Sometimes a patron is too angry for active listening, or paraphrasing, or even "I Believe You" to work. The patron is furious, and wants a chance to express his or her rage to someone from the library. No staff person needs to listen to abusive or obscene language from a library user, but sometimes this kind of anger can be defused by using the "Stand and Deliver Technique." It is called this because the staff person stands there and the patron delivers anger.

The staff person listens attentively to what the patron says, nodding appropriately, and working hard to stay calm and not appear combative. S/he makes no attempt to respond in any way, although s/he may occasionally murmur affirmative sounds, such as "uh huh," and "hmmmm." There is no point in trying to interject information or ask questions, because the patron would simply interrupt if s/he did.

Eventually, the patron will run out of steam. Then the staff person can begin, calmly, to state the library's position on the problem. But it is important here to avoid arguing with the patron. Better is for the staff person to restate the library's position over and over again—like a broken record. The staff person should also try to think up alternatives that will mitigate the situation without violating library policy.

And if it is finally clear that there is no way the staff person is going to be able to get the patron to let go, s/he should refer the matter up the line to his supervisor or the director. Sometimes angry people feel better when they can talk to the "the boss." Anyway, management gets paid more, so why shouldn't they have to handle difficult people too?

One library director points out that the worst problem with angry and verbally abusive patrons is the psychological damage they do to staff. It can take an hour or more for a staff person to recover emotionally from a "stand and deliver" encounter, unless she has learned and incorporated into her consciousness the old Zen lesson: when an insult spear is thrown at you, move you head. One reason for identifying a "handling" technique, and giving it a memorable name, is to help staff objectify the situation—to move their heads instead of getting emotionally speared.

The So Sweet I Can't Stand It Technique

I'm the kind of person who likes to come home at night, pour myself a glass of wine, put my feet up, and spend a quiet half hour with the evening paper. For a long time in Santa Cruz County we had a paper with an evening edition, but alas they had some delivery problems. So every couple of weeks or so, I would come home and there would be no paper on my doorstep. And I would call up Circulation at the paper with steam coming out of both my mouth and my ears, to find out what happened to my paper.

The Circulation Department had the most incredible woman on duty from 4 P.M. to 7 P.M. "Oh, Mrs. Turner," she would all but coo. "Did they miss your house *again*? I'm *so* sorry. I will send a car with it right away. Now you just sit down, put your feet up, and have a nice glass of wine. It will be there before you know it."

There is absolutely nothing you, as an angry person (at least if you have any conscience at all) can say to a response like that. It is a perfect technique to use with people who are mad and have a right to be, but also need to be calmed down.

A Few More Tricks for Promoting Civility at the Front Desk

Periodically we all need to remind ourselves that while it is true that patrons can behave very badly, there are also certain behaviors by public desk workers that invite patron annoyance, and should consequently be avoided by staff at all costs:

- embarrassing an adult in front of his or her children.
- embarrassing a teenager in front of his or her peers (especially his. But girls don't respond well to this treatment either).
- cold and/or marginally hostile demeanor, or simply failure ever to smile.
- inability to make eye contact with the person being served.
- continuing conversations with colleagues while waiting on a patron.
- calling users by their first names when not personally acquainted.
- talking in jargon, e.g., OCLC, LC, periodical, PAC, interface, ISBN, monograph, serial, etc.
- calling anyone younger "honey" or "dear."
- making users feel even sillier than they already do for asking a question.

Looking at the Situation Which Causes Problems

The Memphis–Shelby County staff used the "I Believe You" technique to solve a problem they were having with video collection users. The library used to charge $1.50 to borrow a video for three days, and lots of patrons would bring them back with complaints (the staff thinks because actual cash money was involved): The video wasn't rewound, it didn't work on the patron's VCR, it wasn't the movie the patron thought it was going to be, and so forth. They wanted their money back. But giving a refund for each $1.50, or crediting the borrower account, was far too complicated to be a serious option.

The circulation desk staff thought up this solution. Whenever a patron returning a video complained, the staff person said, "I believe you," and offered the patron a coupon for a one free video checkout. No questions, no arguments.

So lesson one is that well-prepared staff can defuse anger, and get what's wanted even from hostile transactions, if they are clever about it and use the right language.

But lesson two is equally important: A library staff has to be flexible in its approaches to problems. And management has to be willing to evaluate rules, policies, and procedures in terms of real life at the public service desks. Which is more important: maintaining the goodwill of a lot of library users, or extracting $1.50 for every video borrowed? If a well-meant rule or procedure, even a seemingly necessary rule or procedure, is generating a lot of surplus complaints, considering alternatives may be in order—the more creative, the better.

And there is a lesson three in this example: another reason why it is important to cast a fresh eye on "problems" is because sometimes it turns out that they are more apparent than real. This is especially true with ones involving angry patrons, since everyone remembers a loud complaint from a user longer than a grateful smile. Memphis–Shelby County Library had 10,000 coupons printed up when this "I Believe You" strategy was implemented. Over the next ten months the staff distributed an average of 58 coupons per month, which comes out to 2.5 coupons per library branch at a cost of $3.75 per branch. It was a problem that disappeared.

Training staff in problem solving, e.g., thinking up creative solutions to problems we didn't know we had, can be a very useful process. But the most important point here is that while we all know that library users can on occasion be *very* unpleasant, it is nevertheless wise to pay attention to what is making them mad.

There will certainly be things about which the staff can do nothing (at least for the time being). Adding more parking spaces in a crowded downtown is one example. But has the number of "claims returned" complaints been rising recently, as in "I *know* I returned this book just two days ago, honestly!" Wouldn't it be worth at least discussing taking a look at the notice-sending sequence to see if it could or should be lengthened?

Front desk and other staff should be asked to log complaints (an appropriate code system can help make this possible), even the ones they settle happily, just to make sure there aren't things which are falling through the cracks. And if library management is truly interested in finding answers for making library life easier for everyone, the front line staff should also be actively involved in the search for problem solutions.

Ten Minutes a Week for Training

Here are some scenarios that might be used in a staff meeting at which the training topic is handling angry patrons. They envision pairs of staff working together to discuss the problem and propose an effective response.

1. A patron has driven a long way to the library to get a book she really wants, and now learns that you won't check it out to her because it is cataloged for Reference. She says she can't use it here in the library, and gets really mad when you refuse to let her have it. How do you handle this?

2. A line has formed at the checkout desk because you have had to spend a lot of time explaining the rules to a patron who has a lot of overdue materials. The line-waiters are getting increasingly restive. Finally, one of them elbows up to the front and says, "Look, could you just take care of those of us who aren't causing trouble, and make this person wait?" What do you do?

3. "This is one of the worst libraries in [California], as far as I can see," says the man as he passes through the checkout line. "I ask a question about a prescription drug and the bimbo at the Information Desk says she can't look it up because the computer system is down right now. Then I look for a repair manual for my '82 Chevy and the one I need turns out to be missing. So I ask where I can get it, and you say it'll probably take at least a month to borrow it from another library, and you aren't sure you can borrow that kind of book anyway. There might be a wiring diagram on the Internet, but the computer is down. I see you've got all these books in *Spanish*—why don't you get what we need in *English*, that's what I want to know." What do you say?

4. A user objects to the $11.00 fee which has been added to his account for damaging a video's plastic case. He says he could buy a new case for half that amount at the drug store. This fee is highway robbery, and it is totally wrong that the library would be trying to make money off of poor taxpayers, especially since it already gets all that tax revenue. What do you say?

5. The Library recently contracted with a collection agency to go after long-delinquent accounts. Mrs. Fisk is one of them (she owes upwards of $175 in back fines and lost materials). Mrs. Fisk got her Collection Agency letter this morning, and is now on the phone informing you of 1) her outrage at this insult, 2) her absolute innocence of any knowledge about the missing books or overdue fines, 3) her intent to never darken the doors of the library again, and 4) her lifelong friendship with the Editor of the daily newspaper, who will be hearing about this just as soon as she finishes with you. You say what?

Chapter 4

The Nasty Behaviors: Sexual Deviancy, Parental Child Abuse, and Sexual Harassment

Reports of libidinous outbreaks in supposedly staid libraries tend to draw nudges and snickers. Haven't we all—in library school or starting on the job—heard legends about sex in the stacks? Topless readers? Fervent smooching at the homework tables?

But those are activities that, even if embarrassing and angering, are relatively easy to handle so long as they are consensual.

Far worse are the aberrant acts of deranged adults that truly interfere with the rights of others—particularly women and children—to use the library. Parental child abuse is discussed further on in this chapter. First, let's deal with the deviant sexual behaviors that are harrowingly, often criminally inflicted on library patrons and staff.

Interviews with librarians across the country produced a collection of stories—some shocking and some funny—representing an incredible range of experiences. Flashing, peeping, lurking, propositioning and touching—it is all there, a nasty intrusion in almost every librarian's working life.

One of the biggest problems with sexually aberrant behavior is that library workers can become inured to it. A college-aged book shelver may think exhibitionism is so harmless that it isn't worth reporting. And a reference desk worker may feel so embarrassed, or so tired, or so harassed by life in general, that she sees it as "coming with the territory" and too much trouble to fix.

Wrong, wrong, wrong. Part of the training of staff must be learning that *any* kind of sexual harassment is inappropriate behavior in a library, and must be stopped. The book shelver needs to understand that what she may regard as boring could frighten an older patron or a child. And the desk worker should know that she is entitled to better from her work situation than sexual harassment from patrons or colleagues.

As librarians we have virtually no powers to enforce those laws that exist against deviant sexual behavior. Our emphasis therefore must be on *preventing* incidents if we can, dealing with them swiftly when they do occur, and doing whatever we can to help the victims. The focus of this chapter is how we can most effectively deal with the sexual misbehavior of patrons.

First, Some Definitions

The *Diagnostic and Statistical Manual of Mental Disorders(DSM-III-R)*[1] describes four paraphilias (deviations in sexual behavior) which most of us working in public libraries will recognize. Descriptions of each behavior are presented here because one finds this specificity so rarely in library literature. We are all librarians, and of course we can "look it up" if we really need to, but how often do we bother? In fact, though, knowing at least a little about the behavior pathology can give us confidence in dealing with the kinds of problems created for our staffs and our patrons.

Exhibitionism is probably the most common paraphilistic behavior in libraries. An exhibitionist has recurrent, intense, sexual urges to expose his genitals to a stranger. The person may also masturbate while exposing himself. The disorder is apparently confined exclusively to men.

Most crucially, from the library's perspective, an exhibitionist (or "flasher") is *not* likely to be physically dangerous; his intent is to surprise or shock his victim, and he may fantasize that the victim will be sexually excited. But once such a person has acted on his urges, typically there will be no further sexual activity. It is possible, of course, to hypothesize a case in which an exhibitionist has multiple derangements and acts out physically as well. But decades of police experience point the other way, and law enforcement agencies routinely advise their staffs that exhibitionists are nonviolent.

Exhibitionism is frequently summed up as an act designed to draw attention to the exhibitionist. This provides some clues as to how to handle it. For example, there is a frequently told story (surely apocryphal, but amusing anyway) about a stereotypical female librarian of a certain age who was confronted by an exhibitionist at the reference desk.

"Oh, you poor man!" she said to him sympathetically, shaking her head. He zipped up, left the library, and never returned again.

Knowing the exhibitionist is almost surely not dangerous is reassuring information the staff can provide to a patron who reports an incident. It also means that in almost all cases a library staff person need not fear approaching a perpetrator and taking his picture, or asking him to wait in the staff area for the police to arrive. Depending on the situation, these may not be appropriate steps to take, but if taken, in all likelihood the staff person will encounter no personal peril.

Frotteurism and/or Toucherism is rubbing and/or fondling behavior by a paraphile on an unsuspecting, non-consenting person. Usually, this behavior occurs in crowded places, where the person can escape unobserved. But it can and does happen in libraries—in a line at the circulation desk, in a group around the copy machines, and so forth.

The Frotteurist picks a victim who he finds physically attractive, and who may be wearing tight fitting clothes. He rubs his genitals against the victim's thighs and buttocks, or fondles her with his hands. One obvious problem with apprehending and prosecuting a Frotteurist is that characteristic behavior is to escape quickly after touching the victim.

Pedophilia, probably the most frightening sexually deviant behavior in a library setting, is defined as recurrent, intense, sexual urges and fantasies involving prepubescent children (usually those 13 or younger).

> Individuals with Pedophilia generally report an attraction to children of a particular age range. Some individuals prefer males, others females, and some are aroused by both males and females. Those attracted to females usually prefer eight-to-ten-year olds, whereas those attracted to males usually prefer slightly older children. Pedophilia involving female victims is reported more often than Pedophilia involving male victims.[2]

Again, pedophiles are almost always men. Some are attracted to children and to adults, and some only to children. Many pedophiles were sexually abused as children themselves.

Not all pedophiles are child molesters. The definition includes sexual *urges* and *fantasies*, that do not necessarily lead to action. And not all child molesters are pedophiles; sometimes people abuse children because of other mental derangement, or simply out of desire to hurt the child's loved ones.[3]

Libraries unfortunately are prime target zones for pedophiles: men following young girls around, or soliciting boys in the bathrooms or elsewhere. One special problem is the failure of many child victims to report the solicitation or the harassment—out of embarrassment or failure to recognize it. This puts a special burden on staff to maintain alertness.

A *voyeurist* is what in slang we call a "Peeping Tom." A person with this disorder is sexually aroused by observing unsuspecting people who are naked, or getting undressed, or engaged in sexual activities. Usually the people are strangers. A voyeur doesn't seek actual sexual contact with the person observed, but might later fantasize about a sexual experience with the observed person.

Voyeurism is not the same as getting pleasure from watching pornographic films. The voyeurist's sexual arousal is based on secretive, illegal, peeping. Actors in pornographic films or live performances know they are being observed.

In libraries we run into a relatively mild type of voyeurism: men standing underneath an open stair case staring up the skirts of women, or lying on the floor in the stacks, theoretically reading, but actually waiting for an unsuspecting female to come by. Like exhibitionists, voyeurs are not typically dangerous. But they certainly are unpleasant, and they certainly interfere with the right of women and girls to use the library.

Stalking and Staring is not defined by *DSM-III-R* as a paraphilia, but it is a deviancy which is apparently increasing in our society. The most famous cases have involved celebrities, but the vast majority of victims are ordinary people, including library workers. There isn't a well-defined profile of the "typical" stalker, but they do seem to share some characteristics: intense interest in the media, inability to develop meaningful relationships, a history of unsuccessful efforts to establish personal identity, and a strong desire for recognition and attention. Stalkers (and starers, who might escalate to stalking) are dangerous.

Library workers who have been victimized by staring or stalking seem to have suffered most when their supervisors failed to acknowledge the problem, and did not involve the police in stopping it. One reference librarian, for example, was tormented for months by a man who followed her from place to place in the library. She was given some sympathy, but no support or help in stopping his behavior, and only when he began to follow her to the parking lot each evening were the police finally called.

This is absurd. No individual, whether mentally ill or not, has the right to interfere with a woman's right to do her job. Victims of this kind of harassment need to know that they should not feel guilty for resenting deviant behavior, and taking action to stop it. Library managers must take responsibility for training staff in how to cope with such behavior, and for involving law enforcement agencies quickly when confrontation doesn't work.

DSM-III-R categorizes all the other sexual deviancies we encounter in libraries as "Paraphilia Not Otherwise Specified," such as telephone scatologia, which is how psychiatrists talk about obscene phone calls. Practically anything else, from persistent requests for information about nude beaches to masturbating while reading a newspaper, can be put into one of the behavior categories listed above.

Creating a Safe Library Environment

There are several things a library staff can do to create an environment that is less likely to provide opportunities for sexual harassment of patrons. One is to implement as many as possible of the suggestions made in Chapter 8 about safe buildings: insist on good sight lines for staff in any new building, ensure that the restroom entrances are not hidden behind stacks or down dark hallways, and make the restrooms lockable so that staff can control the number of users.

Another is to ensure that all staff are trained to be alert to potential problems ("*Why* is that guy lying on the floor to read?") and to adopt a straightforward attitude toward enforcing the library's rules. If a page sees someone lying on the floor, for example, s/he should be prepared to say, immediately, "I'm sorry, sir, but lying on the floor to read causes a hazard for other patrons. Will you please move to a chair?" It shouldn't be necessary to call in a supervisor before acting, although resistance by the patron or fear on the part of the page obviously would justify this step.

Working with the Police

Establishing a working relationship with local law enforcement officials is particularly well advised in dealing with sexual harassment incidents. It is astonishing how much the police know about what is going on (and who is doing it), and how helpful they can be if the library staff reaches out for assistance.

Reaching out is a means for jumping the real gap that often exists between library staff values (information for everyone, confidentiality above all) and those of the police (our job is to enforce the law, no one knows as much as we do about how horrible people really are). Police officers invited to consult with library staff—to lend their expertise to finding ways to handle problems— develop new understanding of how the library works, why it does what it does, and why its staff seems to be so tolerant of all those "weirdos" who use it. Once achieved at the command level, this is an understanding that will eventually be passed down the ranks within the police force, and will be an enormous help to the staff in the long run.

Among other things, the police can help lay the groundwork for getting permanent restraining or trespass orders against habitual offenders, sexual or otherwise. Another option, again requiring police understanding of the library situation, is to make staying out of the library a condition of probation. The latter usually takes less legal paperwork.

Most important, a police department that knows the staff at the library also knows that the staff will not call unless there is a real emergency or a problem of high priority.

Ensuring the Safety of Children

Providing a safe environment for children involves special problems. A library cannot (and surely doesn't want to) make a blanket rule that forbids adults unaccompanied by children from visiting the Children's Room. Staff also cannot approach people and ask them to leave, based upon their dress or other aspects of their physical appearance. Presence in the Children's Room can be limited to those who are using the children's collection, but this is not a rule all libraries care to make.

What the staff *can* do is keep their eyes open for suspicious behavior, such as a patron gazing steadily at a child who is clearly not a relation, and find a way to interfere. For example, the staff person can approach the starer and say, "Is there something in this collection I can help you find?" Linda Luke of the Alachua County Library in Gainesville, Florida, calls this the "Killing Them with Kindness" approach.

"We don't have a rule forbidding people to use the children's room," she says, "But if we spot someone who is acting like he is after kids, we try to drive him crazy with helpfulness: Can I help you with that computer? Are you sure there isn't something I can find for you? And so forth. It usually works."

Constant vigilance seems to be one key to providing a safe environment for children. Another is ensuring that the staff has its priorities straight. On the one hand, staff should not be so nervous and suspicious that they move on any adult male who dares to show his face in the Children's Room. Ninety-nine percent of all adult and teenaged men are not child molesters or voyeurs. On the other hand, when in doubt, the staff should act on behalf of children, and worry about the rights of adults later.

Boys are the targets of pedophiles as well as girls. But from an early age girls are trained and warned far more frequently about danger from "strangers." Boys unfortunately tend to lack the radar girls develop for sensing inappropriate sexual approaches—and often, as a consequence, have less panache in handling them. There was, for example, the wonderful child in Eugene, Oregon, who was sent off alone to the bathroom by her parent ("*Why* do parents *do* that?" asks the library director) and ran into a man who exposed himself to her.

"The bathroom is over there," she said matter-of-factly, pointing to its door.

A PICTURE IS WORTH...

Polaroid cameras, loaded with film and ready for immediate use, are a handy tool to have in any library's emergency kit. You never know, after all, when an earthquake or hurricane will hit and you have to document the twisted shelving and books on the floor for the Federal Emergency Management Agency when there isn't a drug store open for miles. Polaroid cameras can also be used to back up staff documentation of criminal behavior, particularly sexual harassment.

When an exhibitionist is reported or observed, a member of the staff can immediately spot the perpetrator, and take his picture. The result can be used for identification purposes, to help the police, or simply as an aid for staff on the lookout for someone who is known to prey on children. Using photography can help a library strengthen its reputation as a place where sexual harassment of staff and patrons is *not* tolerated, but it is also a tool that should be used with caution. It is legal to take photographs without the consent of the subject when there are reasonable grounds to believe that the subject is engaged, or was engaged, in criminal behavior. "Reasonable grounds" would be a patron or staff person reporting the incident. Taking the picture may frighten the perpetrator into a hasty exit from the library, but at least the staff then has something to give the police.

It is also very important for the library staff not to fall into the practice of taking pictures of anyone who "looks suspicious," or behaves in an unusual way. Women who wore trousers were once viewed as very suspicious indeed. Access to the information public libraries provide is a basic right of all the people, protected by the First Amendment to the Constitution of the United States. Photography is only appropriate when criminal behavior is being investigated.

Handling Sexual Harassment Situations: Standard Procedures

The cornerstone of any staff response to a report of an incident of sexual harassment in the library must be meeting the needs of the victim. Although it is important to call the police as soon as possible, staff should be trained to give their highest priority to the victim, and let law enforcement worry about catching the perpetrator.

Appendix C offers an example from the Santa Cruz library staff problem situation manual for handling sex incidents. Its advice is pretty standard:

1. Drop everything to pay attention to the victim.
2. Treat the victim with compassion and sympathy.
3. Extract as much information as possible about the incident from the victim.
4. Armed with a description, try to identify the perpetrator. Take a Polaroid picture of him if you can.
5. Call the police and get the victim to file a formal complaint.

When a child reports that she/he has been sexually harassed by someone, or "bothered" by an adult, most manuals advise following the same procedures as those for an adult, modified by the age of the victim, and the presence or absence of the child's parent.

NOTE: Many states *require* that all cases of sexual harassment and sexual abuse involving children be reported by the public official who observes them. Library management should verify whether library workers are included in the definition of "public official" under their own state's law, and the library's procedures should include instructions for staff telling how to do it (e.g., report the incident to the police).

Harassment Not Otherwise Specified

STALKING OR STARING

Most cases of stalking and staring involve a patron abusing a member of the library staff (see the Staff section later in this chapter). But other patrons do occasionally report that they are being harassed in this fashion. The coping techniques are direct, but thy are fraught with the possibility of embarrassment. Suppose, for example, that the person complaining is a zany who fanaticizes about being stared at or stalked. An innocent library patron has a right to feel indignant if he is wrongly accused, and the library might loose him as a customer forever over the incident.

On the other hand, taking a jaundiced view of such a staring complaint is tantamount to blaming the victim, an experience no abused woman deserves. Staff's obligation, in the face of a staring complaint, is to investigate with caution and tact and exercise common sense.

If a patron comes to a staff person and reports that another patron is staring at her, ask the complainant to point out the perpetrator, and get her to describe the behavior factually and clearly.

Suggest first that the complaining patron move to another library table. If she refuses, or says she has already tried that, go with the complainant to the abusing patron and coach her through a confrontation. She should say something like, "When you stare at me, you are harassing me and making it hard for me to read what I came for. You must stop it. Please move to another place to sit. If you don't move, I will ask the staff to call the police."

Staff should make it clear that if the patron does not cease and desist, the police will be called. If the patron doesn't, telephone for law enforcement help.

As the understanding of stalking in the law enforcement and mental health communities has increased (along with media coverage and public awareness), we have all become more conscious of the right of women to be protected from sexual predators of all sorts. But the police cannot act if they do not know about the problem. Library managers should not hesitate to insist on decisive action, including arrest, securing court orders to forbid library use, or continuing protection for the staff person being victimized.

Handling Child Abuse in Libraries

Physical abuse of children, witnessed by staff, and what the staff is supposed to do about it, are phases one and two of a problem situation fraught with difficulties. Issues of local and state law, personal staff feelings of moral outrage, obligation and responsibility, and library confidentiality are all involved. Although child abuse incidents in libraries are seldom sexual in nature, handling them is discussed in this chapter because the typical personal response of the staff—extreme distaste and anger—is much the same as it is to sexual harassment.

Here is a story told by Librarian Meredith Pierce, who works in the children's department of the Alachua County Library in Gainesville, Florida.[4]

Meredith was staffing alone one Saturday afternoon when a woman came in with two children. It was pretty clear that the woman and the little girl, who looked to be three or four years old, were not getting along.

The mother sat the child down in a chair and told her not to move. The child wriggled. The woman snapped her fingers at her several times, and pointed in the direction of the bathroom. The child walked slowly to the bathroom, "her lip sticking out a mile and head hanging," with the woman following.

Meredith felt there was something basically wrong, so after a moment she too followed. As she arrived at the bathroom door, "I heard her striking, I heard the sound of somebody being hit real hard a lot, like maybe eight times, and you know I rushed into the bathroom. There was another child in the bathroom, and it was just a very tense, horrible situation. And I didn't know to what extent I would be allowed to intervene. So by that time she had stopped hitting the child. She was snarling at the child."

Meredith was physically reluctant to get between the woman and the child, but was relieved that at least the mother had stopped hitting. When the woman finally noticed her, Meredith said, "We have a policy of no hitting—no hitting anybody in the library." The woman said, "I am her mother and I will thank you to stay out of this, thank you."

"She was very snippy," says Meredith. "But she *stopped*—my being there stopped her…. She left the restroom…. The child was crushed and sobbing…. I didn't want to do anything to get the library in legal trouble, but I didn't want her to be harming the child."

Meredith didn't have anyone to ask for help at that moment. Later, the woman became all "snuggle bunnies" with her child, "…patting her and chin-chucking her and her little kid was just like in a coma ... crushed and not responding." They left the library, finally, and since they didn't check out any books, Meredith wasn't able to get the name and address. "I had nothing to report," she says.

Meredith later discussed the incident with her manager, who felt that she did not have any choice but to handle the matter as she did. Her presence was enough, they agreed. She didn't *need* to do more because she stopped the behavior, and she *couldn't* do more without interfering in parental control of the child.

Meredith was reassured by this analysis, but remains haunted by the incident. "Parental control of their children is a very fine line. We don't have security cameras in the restroom. I think that's why she took the child in there. And I'm still not quite clear ... if we are allowed to come between parents and the child they're blatantly abusing."

Other librarians report physical abuse incidents which don't even occur in the privacy of the bathroom. "Adults—I assume they are parents—sometimes act as though we are *furniture*," comments one children's room worker. "They do amazing things, like pull a child's arm behind his back, as though we aren't even there. At my library our first strategy is to get them to *notice* us."

The consensus of opinion among children's librarians supports how Meredith handled the incident in Gainesville. The advice is to intervene, but in a way which *objectifies the situation*, using language which is not prejudicial or loaded.

NEVER say "Don't you hit that child. We don't allow child abuse in the library." Instead, say, "We don't allow that behavior in the library," or "We don't allow hitting in the library."

The two-fold point is to get the adult to stop, while not making the physical hostility worse. Also, you don't want the parent to come back at the child later, when you aren't there, with blame that she or he "created a problem for us when we were at the library."

Meredith wonders if there is a hard and fast rule for what action to take, and the answer, apparently, is no, there isn't. Even the legal issues are clouded. For example, as noted earlier in this chapter, many states require that public officials report suspected cases of child abuse. But such legislation is not always helpful. The laws in some states, for example, focus on teachers and day care workers, apparently on the theory that they are the ones who see the same children repetitively, and so are in a good position to spot abuse.

The status of librarians and library workers as "public officials" is very unclear. Can a librarian be prosecuted for failing to report abuse, as a teacher can? Which has priority: reporting suspected abuse, or maintaining patron confidentiality, which is also the law? No one has been willing to give statewide answers to these questions, so procedure is up to local preference.

All libraries should check local and state statutes, and request local interpretation from their legal counsel if necessary, to find out the legal obligations of staff. And they should do it *before* a case of suspected abuse comes up.

Here are two other pieces of advice. Encourage the children's room staff (and all the staff if it turns out to be appropriate) to log incidents of observed child abuse, even if they are not being reported to child protective authorities or the police. This creates a paper record, which can be used in staff training and may be helpful if a legal case needs to be built later. It also helps a staff person recover from the shock and anger of the incident.

Second, children's room and other staff benefit from talking to each other about cases they have observed and how they handle them. A library might find it helpful to ask social workers from a child protective services agency to brief the staff on abuse incidents and frequency in the county, local procedures for handling, and the like.

Physical abuse of children is a problem about which we, as a society, are gaining increasing awareness. Psychologists and other health professionals, in concert with child protective workers, are struggling to find ways to stop what apparently is a growing problem in many communities. Public library staffs can participate in this process by doing what they do most effectively: ensuring that the library's collections include the best and most current information on the topic, and making sure the public at large knows the library has the information.

The best way to do those two things is to work with the professionals who are leading the community's anti-child abuse efforts. They may not have thought of the public library as a place where child abuse happens, or the dilemmas staff confront in handling what they observe. Also, it may not have occurred to them that the public library is a place visited by thousands of adults and children every year. If you remind them of that, they will be very glad to welcome whatever the library can bring to their efforts.

Staff Sexual Abuse

The previous sections of the chapter have dealt with one-one interactions between members of the public. But another issue is staff relationships with one another, and the staff's right to a harassment free work place. That sexual harassment can come from other members of the staff, from the public, or it can come from the circumstances of library work—the public's use of the Internet. The latter is discussed in Chapter 7, which is about all the difficult situations created by Internet access.

To my mind, one of the great achievements of the Women's Movement has been putting the issue of sexual harassment in the workplace into our common consciousness. The unions and others who represent female workers have done as much as Anita Hill to create public understanding that sexual harassment exists—by co-workers, by supervisors, by volunteers—and that women (and men) have a right to work in an environment free of it.

The difficulty is that one person's friendly comment ("You always look great in blue,") is another person's harassment. And what is funny to some people (to men, for example) is offensive to others (to women, for example). The reality is that these days there is no happy medium. The way to avoid the perception of harassment is to eliminate all talk about physical attributes, appearance, and sex from workplace conversations. This of course reduces social intercourse (you should excuse it) to very limited subject areas, but hey, times are tough. Talk about baseball or knitting.

Libraries need to do at least three things to create a harassment-free environment for their workers: develop a discrimination/harassment policy that includes procedures to implement it, train staff, and enforce the policy with vigor.

Discrimination and harassment are linked because they are two sides of the same coin. "Discrimination" includes basing an employment decision on race, sex, age, religion etc. It also includes treating an applicant or an employee differently because of their race, sex, and so forth.

The following definition of "harassment" comes from one municipality's Administrative Procedure Order on the subject, and is quoted at length because it sheds so much light on the issue:

"Harassment" as used in this policy is defined to include, but is not limited to:

A. Speech, such as epithets, derogatory comments or slurs and lewd propositioning on the basis of race, color, creed, national origin, ancestry, religion disability, medical condition (including pregnancy, child birth and cancer-related conditions), gender, weight, physical characteristics, marital status, sex, age, sexual orientation, organizational affiliation, disabled veteran status or status as a veteran of the Vietnam era. Prohibited speech may include inappropriate sex-oriented comments on appearance, including dress or physical features, or race-oriented stories or jokes.

B. Physical acts, such as assault, impeding or blocking movement, offensive touching or physical interference with normal work or movement when directed at an individual.... Prohibited physical acts include pinching, grabbing, patting, propositioning, leering or making explicit or implied job threats or promises in return for submission to physical acts.

C. Visual insults, such as derogatory posters, cartoons or drawings related to the protected bases listed in the policy (e.g. race, sex, religion, etc.).

D. Unwanted sexual advances, requests for sexual favors and other acts of a sexual nature, where submission is made a term or condition of employment, where submission to or rejection of the conduct is used as the basis for employment decisions or where the conduct is intended to or actually does unreasonably interfere with an individual's work performance or create an intimidating, hostile or offensive working environment.[5]

A good policy will start by explaining why sexual harassment is bad: It is against federal, state, and local laws, undermines morale and employee integrity, reduces productivity, and can cause skilled and valuable workers to leave the library's employment. It will then go on to list the unacceptable behaviors by defining both discrimination and harassment as above.

Next, the policy should outline the procedures for handling complaints by people who believe they have been discriminated against or harassed. Typically, these procedures might be as follows:

1. Employee files complaint, including what, when, suspected who, and hoped for remedy. The policy should make it clear that the complaint can be filed with any supervisor of manager—that it doesn't have to go to the employee's particular supervisor. It should also contain the requirement that the Director be immediately notified. Complaints should be in writing. Why? Because having to write it out gives the employee the opportunity to clarify her/his thinking about what happened. But here's an implementation note: if an employee complains orally but can't seem to bring herself or himself to writing it out, suggest that someone (e.g. a co-worker) help.

2. The Library Director conducts an investigation of the complaint. If the allegations prove to be violations of the library policy then the Director takes remedial action, disciplining the at-fault employee.

3. Appeals processes and other remedies driven by collective bargaining contract stipulations should be built into the policy. So should provisions for protecting everyone's privacy.

One of the worst kinds of harassment—and the kind that demands the swiftest action by management—is when a senior worker or a supervisor is accused of harassing a junior employee. Supervisors who approach junior staff with requests for dates or other personal attentions are exploiting their position of authority. They may place the junior person in the position of being unable to respond negatively to the request, for fear of work-related reprisal.

It is therefore critical that the library's policy and procedures make it very clear that sexual approaches by a supervisor are inappropriate management behavior and are subject to disciplinary action.

Training the staff on the Sexual Harassment policy is a matter of making sure everyone has read it, offering special workshops or staff meeting presentations on the subject, and using cases (like the ones at the end of this chapter) as discussion topics at staff meetings. Training issues tend to boil down to two.

The first is getting everyone to understand the basic point that harassment is in the eye of the beholder, and that a sensible worker will learn to avoid remarks about physical appearance, making sexual jokes, and the like.

The second is teaching staff that they do not have to endure sexual remarks from co-workers, and giving them the language to deal with it if it happens. The Santa Cruz Problem Situation Manual (see Appendix C) offers the following set of rules for conduct by library workers, all of which can be discussed and practiced in a training session:

1. If a co-worker or a supervisor makes sexually oriented jokes or comments to you which you consider offensive, tell the person. Say, "I think that remark is inappropriate. Please do not say things like that to me."

2. If the person persists, report the matter to your supervisor. *It is very important that you do this; we cannot create a harassment free environment if people are unwilling to speak out or complain.*

3. If the persisting person is your supervisor, report the behavior to her/his supervisor. Do this immediately. You will be protected. If you feel the supervisor will not handle the matter appropriately, report it directly to the Personnel Department. *Sexually harassing behavior by a manager is inappropriate, and subject to discipline. It cannot be investigated and stopped if it is not reported.*

4. It is absolutely forbidden to use the Library's or the City's electronic mail system for personal use, including messages with sexual content.

5. As a worker or a supervisor, do not comment, joke, or discuss matters with sexual implications (such as dress and appearance) with co-workers. The simplest way to avoid problems in this area is to talk about something else.

Examples of Inappropriate Remarks:

"I like that blouse you're wearing."
"You look great in jeans."
"You look wonderful in blue."
"Curly hair like yours is such a turn on."
"I've always loved guys with mustaches."[6]

As for enforcing the policy with vigor, this means dropping other projects to deal swiftly with a written complaint, documenting the investigation for the Library's confidential files, and imposing disciplinary punishment on people who are guilty of harassing acts. For example, an official written reprimand, coupled with a warning about the consequences of future acts, might be the punishment for a first time offender. Docking pay or termination might be the second punishment. The important point is to create the understanding among all staff that sexual harassment is not tolerated.

Obscene Phone Calls

On television, when the beautiful heroine is being harassed, the script often has the phone ring, the actress answer it, listen, say "Who is this? Who *is* this?", register fear and horror (beautifully), and hang up. She is almost always wearing something you or I would save for a state dinner at the White House.

But wearing evening clothes and whimpering into the receiver isn't how one is supposed to handle an obscene phone call. The best advice, from law enforcement officers, the psychologists, social workers, and teachers who do self-protection and assertiveness training, and everyone else, is to *hang up.* Don't give the person the satisfaction of getting you to listen. Don't do anything. Just hang up.

A library might want its staff to file reports on or log obscene phone calls, in case there is a sudden surge of them, and the police decide to investigate for a pattern. But otherwise, the basic way to handle them is to ignore them.

Stalking or Staring

The coping techniques are direct. First, the staff person should document what is happening. If, for example, she notices a patron staring at her for the second day in a row, she should write it down, noting the previous day's incident, and try moving to another work station if she can. Her object is to create a paper record that can be used with the police and courts if necessary. Of course she should report the staring to her supervisor, who should verify the facts with her or his own investigation. Someone from the staff should attempt to photograph the patron.

Second, the staff person (assisted by her supervisor or colleague) should confront the patron and make clear that his behavior is inappropriate and unacceptable. She should say something like, "When you stare at me, you are harassing me and making it hard for me to do my work. You must stop it. Please move to another place to sit. If you don't move, you will have to leave the library." Make it clear that if the patron does not cease and desist, the police will be called. If the patron doesn't, telephone for law enforcement help.

Other Harassing Approaches to the Staff

On the West Coast an example of this kind of behavior would be a repetitive question from the same patron about the location of nude beaches. In Gainesville, Florida, it was a patron sitting opposite the Reference Desk, making lewd gestures at, and leering and ogling, the librarian working there. He later escalated to verbal obscenities.

As with stalking and staring, the first way to cope with this kind of harassing behavior visited on staff is direct action. The staff person involved, or someone she calls, should tell the patron that he is interfering with the staff person's ability to do her or his job, and must stop immediately. If he won't, the staff will call the police. If he doesn't, do it.

Ten Minutes a Week for Training

Here are some problem situations you might use in training sessions with staff. The first four are meant to refresh workers on the library's standard coping procedures. The fifth is a case that should provoke discussion about how a library staff should handle a situation with sexual overtones involving the potential safety of a child. The last two are about creating a sexual harassment-free work environment for library staff.

1. A patron comes to the desk and reports that a man in the nonfiction stacks has just exposed himself to her. "Oh yeah, him," says your page, who has overheard the patron report. "Don't worry. He does that all the time."

2. In the children's room you observe a young man who doesn't seem to be after any books, but is spending a lot of time moving up and down the stack aisles. You ask if you can help him find something, and he says no. Since Brownie Scout Troop 36 is due to arrive for a "class visit" in fifteen minutes, and you are not going to be able to keep an eye on him for much longer, what should you do?

3. A library patron comes to the main desk and reports that she is being stared at by a scruffy looking guy who she says is "pretending to read." She says she has moved twice, but he keeps following her. You ask her to come and point him out for you. She refuses, saying she just wants to you know what kind of people hang around in the library. What do you do?

4. You are working at the main desk when a man storms into the library and shouts at you, "Where's the @#$%x@#$%^& who tried to attack my daughter! What kind of place is this that you can't even protect little girls from being harassed by monsters. You just sit here and read books all day, am I right?" This is the first you have heard of the incident, although you faintly remember the man as the father of one of your after-school regulars. How should this situation be handled?

5. The branch has several latchkey children, including an eight-year-old girl who frightens you with her obvious need and desire for physical affection.

You don't know what is going on at her home, but you are disturbed by the way she will talk with anyone, male or female, who shows any kindness to her. Yesterday you saw her being "petted" by a man who you are sure she doesn't know. You stopped that incident by distracting the child, but now you wonder what you should do to find a permanent resolution to a situation you are sure is leading to some sort of disaster.

6. You are conducting an "exit interview" with Debbie, a library clerk who has unexpectedly resigned. "Why are you leaving?" you ask. "You've done an awfully good job, and we'd love it if you stayed." "I just can't stand it anymore," says Debbie. "Stand what?" you ask, and it finally emerges that Bill who works on the Reference Desk has been pestering her for dates, calling her at home, and sending her dirty jokes by email. "I've told him I'm not interested—I have a boyfriend, you know—but he just won't stop. So I think I should just leave and try my luck somewhere else." "Why on earth didn't you report this to me months ago?" you ask. "Well, I thought it's his word against mine, he's the professional, and I ... well, I was embarrassed by the whole thing. I was sure you'd think it was my fault." What's wrong here, and how could this situation have been avoided?

7. Jim, who is openly gay, has worked for the library for five years. He is popular with his co-workers, and very competent in his reference service job. Two months ago he and his partner had a commitment ceremony to which Jim invited his friends on the staff. Several library staff members attended and had a good time, but two or three others found themselves unable to accept this clear statement of Jim's lifestyle, and decided not to go. Shortly thereafter, Jim began to find what could only be described as "poison pen" notes on his desk. Never signed, they were clearly homophobic, using gross language to castigate Jim and his partner for their lifestyle. One of the notes blasted the library's policy of making health benefits available to spouse-like partners and another (incredibly) accused Jim of spreading AIDS through the library staff. Jim was going to leave the whole matter alone, hoping it would go away if ignored, but now he has begun to get anonymous phone calls at home. What should he do? And what should the Library do?

Chapter 5

"It's Free and It's Safe"—Handling Problems with Unattended Children

I was on an airplane flying from Hartford to Chicago one day, compressed into one of those ever-shrinking three-seat rows, when I was saved from existential misery by the discovery that my seatmates—a married couple—were strong supporters of their local county public library. She taught first grade in the local schools, and he, a retired school principal, was the chair of the local library commission.

Since we all came from the same state, we managed to fill the hours of involuntary physical proximity with a lively discussion of automation system installations, plans for their new library building, and the recent sins of the parsimonious state legislature. Their county is a very rural one (33,000 people in more than 1,000 square miles), so I was surprised when one of them remarked that a reason they were so desperate for a new building was the fact that mobs of elementary school kids flooded the existing library every afternoon after school.

"You mean you have a problem with latchkey children," I said.

"Well," one said, "I don't know if I'd call it a problem, exactly, but we do have a lot of kids with no place to go when school gets out, so they come to the library. Childcare isn't any better in rural areas than it is in downtown Los Angeles, you know. In fact, it's probably better in L.A. where at least they have some resources."

"Unattended" (or as they used to be called, "Latchkey") children—subteens whose parents require them to spend significant time at the public library after school in lieu of daycare—and the problems they create for libraries, have been a hot issue at library conferences and in the library press since the early 1980s. While after school use by kids is not exactly new (when did any of us go to the public library except after school?), the number of parents relying on the library to provide a safe refuge for their children (whether the kids like it or not) has definitely increased.

One part of the "unattended kids" situation presents itself merely as a specialized component of the overall task of providing library services to children, and this chapter reflects that fact at certain points of analysis and suggestion: the information needs of unsupervised kids are no different than those of other children. And library rules regarding behavior of unattended kids are the same rules that apply to behavior of, say, children turned loose in the building by a parent who then becomes unresponsively absorbed in personal reading, or kids who come to the library unaccompanied because their parents, at home, trust them to do the right thing when they get there.

But in its larger implications, the unattended problem extends well beyond the routine of children's services. Security, protection, and emergency medical potentials related to latchkey kids are particularly acute and troublesome. So are the overcrowding, abuse of facilities, and impossible demands on staff resulting from the increase in these rootless afternoon youngsters.

Changes in society and the economy have brought us this problem. Politicians who say that it's not the role of government or the schools to provide daycare, or that there aren't enough resources, need to take cognizance of a painful fact: a hidden, increasingly stressful part of most library budgets and staff workdays is being devoted to the afternoon supervision of children whose parents can't find or can't afford other options, and who know that the library is both free and safe.

Unattended Children in the Public Library: A Resource Guide is the title of the updated version of ALA's original 1988 document on the subject, called *Latchkey Children in the Public Library: A Position Paper,* prepared by the Library Service to Children Committee and Public Library Association.[1] It is a highly useful run through the issues surrounding setting policy and implementing programs. Among other things, it points out that the term "latchkey children" seems to cast blame on children for their situation, so these days the term to use is "unattended" or "unsupervised." I don't necessarily agree, but I try to adopt the "correct" terminology when I can.

The *Resource Guide,* as well as a variety of periodical articles in library and popular literature, identify changing demographic factors as the principle reason why there are more unattended children than there used to be. These factors include more women in the workforce, more single-parent, female-headed households, fewer adults available to care for children in their neighborhoods, lack of accessible and affordable child care, and an increase in the number of homeless families with children.

The fact that parents regard the library as a suitable place for their children to spend after-school hours is, of course, to some extent a compliment. After all these years of librarians' work to provide a warm and welcoming atmosphere, offering important intellectual resources for children, many parents have gotten the message.

But, to the extent that the public library is once again regarded as the community's dumping ground for a social problem no one wants to spend the money to solve (see also libraries as day centers for street people), it is infuriating. It is so maddening, in fact, that it is easy to relish the acerbic words of the library world's resident iconoclast, Herb White: "Hospitals also serve children; why don't the kids go there after school? Certainly in part because hospitals won't have them.... Because we have allowed ourselves to be so trivialized, the library can be seen simply as a handy place to come in out of the rain."[2]

But "trivialized" is the wrong word. Cutting through the rhetoric, the angst, and perhaps a tendency to feel sorry for ourselves, let's try, if we can, to get to the heart of the matter.

All children have information needs. Some children have shelter needs outside the home. The library's job is to meet the information needs. It is not the library's job to provide shelter. But taking those needs apart can be very difficult. Many libraries find themselves forced to shelter school-aged youngsters for part of every day in order to meet their information needs. Almost the only way to prevent parents from imposing shelter demands on libraries is to ban all children between the ages of six and twelve from 2:30 P.M. to 5:30 P.M. on weekdays. One's suspicion is that if a library actually announced it couldn't handle the demands being placed on it, and *closed* during the after school hours, the community would quickly manage to find an alternative child care solution.

I believe that the dimensions of most libraries' "unattended kids" problems depend on the size of their staff and budget, and the amount of space in their buildings. Now honestly, isn't it true? Suppose your library had enough money to hire professional librarians and support staff at a ratio of one for every seven or eight kids hanging around in the afternoon, *and* you had enough space to give every child a chair, a table with a computer, a cubby for his/her lunch box, and room on the floor for creative lying around. Would you still regard unattended kids as a problem?

I bet you wouldn't. You'd be too busy thinking up just the right book for Manuel to read, or finding a volunteer to help Marcia with her arithmetic. You'd be looking forward, as the kids are, to the next chapter in whatever book you're reading aloud. You wouldn't care a whit whether combined information and shelter services in the afternoons for youngsters is a proper function of the public library.

But this is a fantasy, of course. None of us have that kind of money, not even the libraries with successful after school programs. Financial reality forces us to limit our services. It is what we agree those limits should be, and how we go about enforcing them, that is the real question. And making sensible "limit" decisions is only possible when a library has engaged in a serious planning process.

Who Are the Latchkey Children?

Back in 1988 *Latchkey Children in the Public Library* identified three main categories of children using the library after school:

> those who choose to frequent the public library because of personal, natural affinities for the library environment;
>
> those who live nearby and go to the library because it is preferable to being at home alone after school;
>
> those children who are instructed to use the library as a shelter by parents and guardians who are unable to provide alternative care for them.[3]

It went on to quote the San Marino, California, library's definition:

> A Library Latchkey child is one who on a regular basis is required by his/her parent or guardian to remain at the public library for extended periods of time after school in lieu of day care. "Regular basis" is defined as three or more days per week. "Extended period" is defined as two or more hours per day.[4]

Please note the modifier "library" associated with the word "latchkey." The children who come to the library are only a *fraction* of those who spend their after school hours unsupervised. The rest are at home alone, on the street, hanging around at the shopping mall, at the houses of friends (where they also may be unsupervised), and who knows where else, courting trouble in the cracks between schools and the general society which apparently does not care about their situation.

It is perhaps useful to further clarify the definition by dividing unattended children into age groups.

Preschoolers left without parental supervision present special problems: they are not old enough to be left alone at the library, any more than they are old enough to be left alone at home. Many libraries have therefore adopted rules that require parents or guardians to stay with their children when they are in the library.

Some go on to define a minimum age for the "guardian" or caregiver, in order to prevent underage siblings from bringing their charges to the library and then leaving them in the staff's care. Babysitter sisters and brothers who are too young for the job (regardless of the cultural traditions of their families), become the source of problems for staff, forcing intervention when inappropriate or abusive behavior develops.

Most working children's librarians urge swift action when parents disobey the "unattended" rule with very young children: Find the parent and tell them directly that they may not leave their preschooler alone in the children's room or anywhere else in the library.

Older children are "unattended" when their parents have left them to find books or whatever for themselves while the parents do other errands or use the adult collection. They are not a problem until their behavior interferes with other people's rights to use the library.

And there are the true unattended kids who meet the San Marino definition: *School aged youngsters* sent to the library by a parent in lieu of some other day care arrangement.

Service Responses and Policies

The policy arguments libraries get into as they confront the "unattended children" problem are a classic example of failure to define service roles and set clear boundaries around them. This was one of Herb White's messages in the article featuring his famous suggestion that kids could go to hospitals after school. Too often we have shouldered the burden of a community problem, simply because it has been thrust upon us, instead of saying loudly and clearly, "No, we are *not* in the child shelter business, and we are not going to be everybody's free after school child care facility."

Most documents being written by American Library Association committees and divisions rest on the premise that every public library is different, and should endeavor to serve different communities. National standards are inappropriate in making plans and designing services. The local library needs to study its community to find out its characteristics, its desires, and its information needs. Then the library should assess which of those needs it can try to meet.

This concept flows from the observation that the demands for service from public libraries are exceedingly diverse, very complex, and frequently conflicting. Libraries traditionally have tried to be all things to all people. But this is an impossible task, and thus public libraries should choose and limit their efforts to services that match their resources with the unique needs of their communities. PLA's *The New Planning for Results, a Streamlined Approach* is a highly useful guide to the process of assessing community need, articulating a community and library vision, and selecting library responses to meet the needs.[5]

If a public library decides that it must build a service response around the needs of children, then it must go on to identify the details of what those needs are and design programs to meet them. The library can and should be assisted in this process by other community groups serving children: the schools, the voluntary service agencies targeting families and children, the boys' and girls' clubs, scout organizations, and the like. This planning process is a golden opportunity for library staffs (and boards) to involve other provider agencies, and politicians too, in explicating real needs, and understanding what the library can and cannot do to meet them. The object is to get the community to agree that the problem requires a collective response. *Unattended Children in the Public Library: A Resource Guide* offers a particularly useful chapter on this subject called "Forging Working Relationships Between Public Libraries and Community Organizations" by Joan Costello and Beatrice Julian.[6]

Components of an Unattended Children Policy

Most good policies have an introduction that clarifies the need for the policy, a problem definition, a statement of the policy itself, and procedures for staff implementation. Whatever model the library uses, the document that is the basis for staff work and public understanding of the library's response to the needs of children unattended after school should contain:

- a clear and positive statement of what the library's services to school aged youngsters will be, and
- a clear and positive statement of what the responsibilities of parents must be.

The policy will also have procedures appended, although these might more usefully reside in the larger staff "problem situations" manual.

Problems and Procedures to Help Handle Unattended Kids

Obviously, it is the children who meet the San Marino definition who cause problems, among other reasons because of the involuntary nature of their presence. Kids who *want* to be at the library are our favorite patrons. And those who choose us over other alternatives will probably do okay most of the time. It is those children who are sent to the library for daycare who most often create difficulties for under-funded and under-staffed public libraries.

There seem to be four major problems created by school aged unattended kids: liability, child security, disruptive behavior, and inappropriate use. The last two in particular are exacerbated by the problem of too little space.

LIBRARY LIABILITY

Here are some of my worst library latchkey fantasies: that a child will be snatched from the library steps and subsequently molested by a sexual deviant. Or that a seven year old will trip and crack her head on the lobby floor: She is unconscious, we've called for emergency help, and no one knows how to reach her parent. Or that a child will be kidnapped from the children's room by a parent involved in a custody fight, and the library will be sued by the other parent. Are libraries legally responsible (i.e., liable) for the physical safety of kids who use them after school? The legal answer is, as usual, murky. We know that public libraries as institutions do not have the legal 'provision of care' responsibilities mandated for schools. And we know that a library staff member should never, ever drive a child home in his or her own car. But aside from these two rules, no legal issues are certain or uniform in all states or localities.

The library's best protection from legal liability, although *not* from lawsuits (which litigious people can and will file for purely arbitrary reasons) are statements of responsibility and behavior rules for parents and children written with the same care as those written for other users (see Chapter 1).

The library staff's best approach to the liability issue is to consult with local counsel and appropriate risk managers when they formulate their policies regarding children. And if these advisers (harassed, perhaps, by the cost of "deep pocket" lawsuits and self-insurance premiums) give advice that is too conservative to allow the library to do its job, then try getting more guidance (re other case law, for example) from ALA's Association for Library Service to Children and the PLA Service to Children Committee.

SECURITY

The security issue arises when a parent has not picked up a child by the time the library closes. Or suppose there is a community disaster or a fire that forces the building to be evacuated and closed. A library needs to establish a procedure for what it is going to do when this happens, so that staff are not left to make up solutions on the spot. And the procedure needs to take into account the age of the child and the location of the library.

Library staff members are not going to be willing to abandon a seven year old on the front steps on a winter evening at 6 P.M. But leaving a twelve year old to his or her own devices is a bit more acceptable, depending on the library's neighborhood, of course. Many libraries instruct staff to take abandoned children to the local police station, or to call the police for a pick up. This doesn't work, however, if the library branch is in a rural area, the sheriff is miles away, and the patrol will thus be a long time in coming. One solution is for the rural branch manager to work out an "abandoned child" arrangement with whatever other government agency is available—for example, the local fire department.

We all know that disasters happen to adults: a terrible accident has blocked traffic for hours and miles, the bus is late, the office caught on fire. Therefore compassion and sympathy should certainly be our attitude. But the parent who gets into this kind of mess, and can't make it to the library by closing time, is forcing the library staff to pay a penalty for his/her decision to use the library for shelter services. The parent should not be doing that, and he or she should be confronted with the truth, using language, such as "child abandonment" or "child neglect" which will make the mistake crystal clear.

Disruptive Behavior and Inappropriate Use

The philosophy behind making behavior rules for kids should be the same as for adults: no one has the right to interfere with anyone else's right to use the library. And in terms of that philosophy, it doesn't much matter whether a child is with a parent or in the library on his/her own. In either case kids can behave beautifully, or like monsters. The library staff needs to think through what its space will accommodate, and what other users can tolerate. For example, a children's room in the basement or isolated on the second floor can probably take more noise than one that is adjacent to the main adult reference area. And the staff of a severely overcrowded facility is obviously going to be less tolerant of collective homework doing or other talking than one with a lot of space.

Young people, especially as they reach sixth grade, are increasingly likely to use the "adult" areas of the library too, where their behavior may need to conform to more stringent rules against talking, snapping bubble gum, and generally annoying other people. Judith Drescher, at the Memphis–Shelby County Library and Information Center, reports that the largest number of problem situations her staff encounters at the headquarters library are complaints from adults about the presence and behavior of kids. It is not that the kids are bad, so much as that there are a lot of them, after school, in a too-small space. Among other things, the Memphis staff tries to advise adults of when the library is less likely to be a youth heaven, e.g. in the morning, while kids are in school.

Here is how the Santa Clara County (California) Library states its behavior rules for young users:

> Appropriate activities include: doing homework, writing reports, researching, browsing for books, thinking, daydreaming, and reading. If games, puzzles, or listening tables are available, they are to be used quietly so as not to disturb others.
>
> Inappropriate activities include: running, throwing, eating, loud or abusive talking, fighting, moving furniture, excessive socializing, or any other activities which disrupt the library. Vandalism will not be tolerated.[7]

And of course, as with all rule enforcement, success is based on the ability to be flexible. The Santa Cruz Library System has a small branch in the redwoods of the coastal mountains. The coach at the local high school likes to assign his track team to a five mile training run in which the halfway point is the branch. The runners pant up the steps and into the library (which is only one room), where they must get a library stamp on the back of their hand from the desk worker to prove they did the whole run. Then they are out the door on the back-to-school leg. As after school support for local kids, I think this one has a certain charm, even if the behavior does violate several standard library rules (no running, no heavy breathing), and also interferes with the right of anyone standing at the circulation desk to complete a book checkout while the track team is visiting.

Procedures for handling all these problems need to be developed with the participation of the staff doing the job. Appendix C has an example of both policy and procedures from the Duluth (Minnesota) Public Library.

Getting the Message Out

Having gone to the trouble of thinking through the library's response to the issue of library services to unattended kids, as well as other services to children and young adults, the library's next task is to inform the public about it. It is especially necessary to tell parents about the policy and program. Here are some ideas for doing that.

1. *Send Home a Letter.* Many libraries require a parental signature on a child's borrower card application, and many don't. In either case, a youngster getting a library card creates an ideal opportunity for the staff to tell parents about the library's services to children, and its rules. This can be done via a letter mailed to the parent or guardian at the child's home address, or by handing it to the parent on the spot. Included in the letter should be a statement of parental responsibility when the child is in the library, and (if appropriate) the library's refusal to provide ongoing shelter services.

2. *Put Out a Leaflet.* Keep on hand a standard flyer describing services to children and listing rules. This can be given to violators, or to anyone who asks.

3. *Post the Unattended Child Rule.* Regardless of where the library stands in the posting rules debate (see Chapter 1), it should at least post the rule about how parents must accompany their children. And, it should post it in the adult areas of the library, as well as in the children's room.

4. *Try to Interest the Media.* The best kind of coverage is a long feature article and a television story about library efforts to meet the information needs of school-age children, including those left on their own after school. If stories

like these can't be finagled, try to get the local press interested in the larger problem. Produce other service providers for a joint press conference. Get the Mayor to declare a Kids on Their Own Day. The point in this is to put across the message that after school care is a community-wide responsibility. The library is doing its part, but it can't carry the whole burden, and so forth.

5. *Work with the Local Schools.* Sure, sure, you're thinking. We always want to work with *them,* but they never want to work with us, except of course when a teacher wants to bring a class to visit, or they've closed the school media center in the latest budget crunch, and we're expected to pick up the slack. And *why* can't they let us know when they assign a whole class to a topic such as astrobiology, about which we have only three books, all of which were checked out by the early birds.

Frankly, I don't have a great deal of sympathy for the trials and tribulations of school staffs—especially for those staffers who obviously don't have any sympathy for the lot of the working librarian. Why is it, for example, that school in the United States ends at 2:30 or 3 in the afternoon? In Europe and Japan children go to school until 5 P.M. or later. But this is a personal prejudice, no doubt informed by the fact that I have never been a teacher, and by my knowledge that we wouldn't have an "unattended children" problem, library or otherwise, if the public schools were organized as full day operations.

So ignore this clear bias. Instead, focus on the number one priority in working with the schools, whether it is meeting the needs of their teachers, or trying to develop a community response to the unattended children problem. This is to make the dimensions (and limits) of public library service clear, and stick to the rules we make to express those limits. If we say an appointment is required for a class visit, then we should refuse to provide special services to a teacher and her twenty students who turn up without one. And we should report habitual offenders (a teacher who does this more than once) to the school principal. If we don't do this, neither the schools nor anyone else are going to take our parental responsibility and other rules seriously.

The second step is to get a little back from the schools, such as space for articles in the Parent Teacher Association newsletter, and a message home for every child at the beginning of each new school year. The letter can be the same as the one delivered when children apply for borrower cards: a welcome to the public library, a description of library services, an explanation of the library rules, and a clear statement of the library's "unattended children" policy.

Latchkey Programs That Work

Frances Smardo Dowd's book, *Latchkey Children in the Library & Community*, offers descriptions of several successful programs, as well as a comprehensive list of latchkey organizations and agencies, and an excellent annotated bibliography.[8] PLA's *Unattended Children in the Public Library* summarizes the various types of programs offered and includes a nifty list called "Fifty Ways to Love Your Unattended Children."[9]

The most interesting thing about all these programs is their incredible diversity. They range from bookmobile service at private care centers to the "Grandparents and Books" programs that seek to link lonely older people with kids in need of after school support. Homework centers, often assisted by volunteers, are a popular and successful program. Frequency ranges from regular daily service to once-a-week special programs. Librarians have coped by opening their meeting rooms and adding vending machines in the lobby so kids have access to snacks.

Many library staffs, especially those from the larger library systems, have taken on the advocacy function, endeavoring to organize community-wide responses at the same time that they run after-school programs in their own facilities. The need to find services for latchkey children is an excellent example of the kind of institutional networking all public libraries are increasingly required to do.

Ten Minutes a Week for Training

Any children's staff endeavoring to serve library latchkey kids is surely doing its own planning and training exercises on the special issues of how to "do it good." It is important to remember, though, that the adult services staff also interacts with kids, and may need special coaching in how to do this effectively. Here are some questions and problem examples that might be used to provoke a discussion aimed at consciousness raising and training. Remember that these training exercises are all intended to remind staff of what your library's standard rules are.

1. Mrs. Jones storms up to the adult reference desk and demands that you "do something" about that group of giggly girls over in the corner. What do you say and do?

2. It is 6 P.M. and closing time. It is also raining and dark. Michael, who is eleven, is still hanging around at the front entrance. You ask how he is going to get home, and he says his dad is picking him up. "What time?" you ask. "Oh, I guess about five," says Michael. What do you do?

3. "Mrs.," says a child approaching you at the Desk. "Nancy is being sick awful bad in the bathroom." You investigate and find that indeed Nancy is vomiting and probably has a fever. And yes, she is on her own at the library. Her mother is at work, and her dad is not at home either. What's next?

4. Again and again the children's room staff have told Mrs. Smith that she cannot tell her youngsters to go to the library every day after school, and wait until she gets off work to pick them up. She says she is a single parent with no money and has no choice. The children are rarely troublesome, but keeping them occupied is requiring a lot of staff attention. What are the staff's options here?

5. The Mayor (who is a reliable library supporter, but at the moment is running in a hard-fought race for reelection) is speaking at a candidate forum. In response to a question, she suggests that parents who can't afford after school care for their youngsters send their kids to the public library. "It's free," she says, "You're already paying for it. And it's safe." What should the director do?

Chapter 6

Censorship: Wizards, Sex, and Killing Animals

I would love to meet J.K. Rowling sometime, and find out whether she ever imagined that her Harry Potter series would top the list of books most challenged by censors four years in a row. Objections to the series from parents and others relate to its focus on wizardry and magic. I always thought the books were (among other things) a wonderful send-up of the British public school system, and the wizards, magic, and stuff a great way to tell an exciting adventure story. Oh well. There is no accounting for taste or prejudice, is there?

The "most challenged" list is produced annually by the American Library Association's Office of Intellectual Freedom (OIF), which reported in January 2003 that challenges to materials in libraries, schools, and school libraries have gone up 15 percent between 2001 and 2002. And these are only the challenges in which a formal, written complaint was filed. Director of OIF Judith Krug says that for each challenge reported, four or five others remain unreported.[1]

A *challenge* to a book or other item is an attempt to remove it (or ban it) from the library shelves or from the school curriculum. A challenge is not the same as a *question or discussion* about a title. A challenge seeks to impose the opinion of an individual or group upon the larger community by restricting access. A question may sound at first like a challenge, but is usually an expression of a user's desire for information. While library workers need to be prepared to deal with both questions and formal challenges, it is important to note that the former are far more frequent and likely occurrences.

The vast majority of the people who raise questions (and ultimately may make formal challenges) about books are doing so because they want to protect others, especially children, from ideas and information they regard as difficult or dangerous. The Office of Intellectual Freedom reports that the top three reasons for challenging materials are that it is "sexually explicit," contains "offensive language," or is "unsuited to the an age group."

It used to be that all questions from the public about materials were automatically assumed to be hostile and challenging. The response forms libraries kept on hand for these emergencies had names such as "Materials Reconsideration Request." The assumption was always that the patron wanted the book removed. The burden of the form (aside from bibliographic identification of the item) was finding out whether the patron represented him or herself, or (oh no, now we're in for trouble) an organization.

These days, the attitude isn't so automatically defensive. It is not that librarians are agreeing to remove materials, so much as that they have begun to recognize that many people who question a title, really only want to talk with someone about it.

Experience shows that there are significantly different types of complaints in this category of librarians' woes. Publicity goes to the ideologues: individuals and organizations demanding that a book be removed or its location in the collection changed, or that censors should scour our public and school library collections of any materials at variance with their own beliefs.

But many of the people who file such complaints or ask such questions (lots of libraries now take these on "comment forms") are like the man who objected to a cassette tape of ghost stories which had scared the dickens out of his five year old. The cassette package was clearly marked, "Ages Nine Years Old and Up," and what the man *really* wanted to talk about was how to choose recorded stories and books for his little boy.

A traditional review of the complaint would have involved looking up the reviews and citing them in a letter explaining the *Library Bill of Rights* and why this specific item met various library selection criteria. And all that work would have missed the point.

But the librarian responding to the complaint form took a better tack. First, she called the parent, learned that the real problem was the age of the child, and that what the father needed was advice. They had an interesting conversation about what kids of five like to read and hear, and both were happy. The library "closed the case" with the staff person writing the patron a short letter saying she had been glad to talk with him.

Library procedures for handling complaints or questions about materials need to address *both* levels of challenge: attempts to "purify" the collection, and the more mundane concerns of worried library users that perhaps can be addressed by explanation or conversation. Procedures also should allow for the fact that not every professional librarian selecting materials is available to talk to the public every minute of the day, and that therefore the commenting patron's first encounter may well be with a member of the library's support staff. But before creating these procedures, the library needs to make sure it has its basic principles and policies in place and in writing.

Creating an Environment of Intellectual Freedom

The American Library Association's Office of Intellectual Freedom, as well as the intellectual freedom committees of the state library associations, provide solid guidance to libraries in creating what they call "environments of intellectual freedom" (i.e., free speech). ALA's *Intellectual Freedom Manual*, 6th Edition, is a truly comprehensive resource which should be on the shelves of every library in the United States.[3] Based on those references, this chapter summarizes some basic groundwork any library must do, and then gets on to its major focus—enabling staff to handle complaints or questions about library materials.

First you need to get your intellectual freedom ducks in order, as it were, by creating a comprehensive materials selection, or collection development, statement (also called a program, policy, or plan). The *Intellectual Freedom Manual* suggests that this document should reflect the library's investigation of its community and its needs, and the library's objectives, geographic environment, and the current collection.

But the basic point is to *write* it, make it official. The statement should be organized in two parts. Part One is the policies: what and why the library does what it does. Part Two contains procedures: how the library does it. The *Manual* makes the point that even the smallest public library needs to take the time and trouble to get this information written down—otherwise, it can make only the poorest of defenses against challenges.

The policy part of the statement sets out the library's understanding of its institutional mission and objectives, and the commitment of its governing authority and staff to the principles of the *Library Bill of Rights* (see Appendix A).

This section also needs to specify the objectives of the library's collection (what user needs is the collection endeavoring to meet?), who is responsible for selection (e.g. the director, who delegates to the professional staff), and the criteria the staff will use in making selections (artistic or literary excellence, appropriateness to level of user, authenticity, interest, cost, review recommendations, etc.).

Finally, the policy statement should tell patrons how the library handles controversial material, starting with the governing authority's commitment to the *Library Bill of Rights*. There are five additional Interpretations of this document that relate directly to selection of library materials, and five more that concern collection access. The latter in particular include important principles about information for children. All these documents are printed and explained in the *Intellectual Freedom Manual*.

Part Two of the Materials Selection Statement should contain specific information about how the library implements the policies set out in Part One: what selection aids the staff will use, how it will handle gifts, procedures for managing special collections, and collection maintenance issues—review of existing materials, weeding, and the like.

Part Two should also include a detailed explanation of how the library will handle questions about or challenges to library materials: the name of the form the patron fills out, what the staff person who receives the form does with it, which professional library position handles the comment, the appeals process, and so forth. A typical sequence of events and a form are included in the Santa Cruz Library Problem Situation manual in Appendix C. The *Intellectual Freedom Manual* devotes a whole chapter to the ins and outs of conducting this process properly and productively. One particularly important point is that the process should be objective, fair, honest, and open.

> The review procedure, including the written questionnaire [materials comment form], should be designed not only as a defense against potential censors, but also as a means to facilitate constructive dialogue. While these procedures do offer the library a defense against arbitrary attacks, they should never be permitted to degenerate into a bureaucratic smokescreen. In a word, the library should welcome constructive input even as it maintains firm barriers to censorship.[4]

The materials selection statement that is the result of all these elements is inevitably long and complex. That's why I am convinced that the *Library Bill of Rights* should be the lead document, always cited first, in any question about selection of materials. Its principles are basic, it has a good title, and it is shorter:

> Books and other library resources should be provided for the interest, information, and enlightenment of all people of the community the library serves. Materials should not be excluded because of the origin, background, or views of those contributing to their creation.

> Libraries should provide materials and information representing all points of view on current and historical issues. Materials should not be proscribed or removed because of partisan or doctrinal disapproval.[5]

See Appendix A for the complete text.

Handling Comments About Materials— The First Round

So we all read the *Intellectual Freedom Manual*, and follow its advice about devising a process for handling challenges. And then we come up against the fact that 99 percent of the situations invoking these carefully crafted procedures end before they ever reach the library director, let alone the library board. That's why it is so important to train all staff in how to respond.

A very wise person once observed that a lot of time is wasted answering questions that were never asked. The trick in handling a question about library materials is to find out what the person *really* wants to know: why did the library select this particular book or other item? Why does the library buy books on this subject? Why is this book shelved in the "easy reader" section of the children's room? Does the library have any other books by this author? and a hundred other variations on the theme.

Most people (other than zealots) who raise questions about a book or other item don't think of themselves as censors and they don't believe in censorship. "Censorship" is a bad word in most Americans' vocabulary—a fact that should reassure any library worker responding to such a challenge. Most "censors" simply don't like a specific item, and want to be able to tell somebody (i.e. a library staff person) what they think about that terrible book, magazine, or video.

As one librarian put it, "Dealing with book complaints is a *service* we provide the public." And, added another, it is a service we should train our staffs to do as well as any other we provide.

Gordon Conable (who is a former library director and is also the long-term President of the Freedom to Read Foundation) suggests that if you think of a book query as a request for service, instead of a complaint, it is a lot less paralyzing. Handling it requires the same skills as those used in a reference interview. You want to extract the real question from the patron via active listening and open-ended questioning.

Doing it well also requires practice. That's why it is very important to take the time at regular staff meetings to role-play encounters between public desk workers and patrons asking questions. See the *Ten Minutes a Week for Training* section at the end of this chapter for some question ideas.

Appendix C, which is the Santa Cruz Library Problem Situation Manual, contains an example in the section called "Book Complaints and Questions about Library Materials" of a conversation between a library user and a staff member. The staff member tries to use her training in active listening to handle the problem. Alas, however, the user is so concerned about his own point of view (he is a vegetarian, and thinks it is wrong that the library has books advocating cooking meats, which encourages children to kill animals) that he doesn't want to listen. It is a true story, and it should be taken seriously as an example even though it doesn't deal with wizardry, sex, or even profanity.

The staff's objective in handling a complaint like that one is to ensure that the person making the comment gets the chance to talk out what she or he thinks. If the patron can't do it right then, he needs to give enough information so that a member of the professional staff can get back to him. Best would be a Comment Form, but in a pinch, the name and phone number will do. The patron also needs to be given a brief rendition of the library's procedures for selecting materials, and for handling complaints about them.

The librarian who follows up on this kind of query will telephone the patron, talk about the question or complaint, and if the patron hasn't already filled out a Comment Form making an "official" comment or complaint, send him one. The librarian would write a response letter which includes a restatement of the *Library Bill of Rights* and other appropriate principles, information on the place the item has in the library's collection development plan, and citations of reviews used when the item was originally evaluated. The letter would also tell the patron what to do next if she wishes to take the matter further. The next step is usually an appeal to the library director.

Good record keeping is essential in this process. A copy of the original Comment Form, as well as the staff response letter or phone call notes should immediately be placed in a central file, where it is accessible to the director or other staff who may need it if the patron isn't satisfied.

Confronting a Censorship Attempt

One time out of fifty (or maybe even a hundred) a patron or an organization will be really angry that the library has a book like *Daddy's Roommate* by Michael Willhoite in the children's collection. Not satisfied with the letter received from the selection librarian, or the result of an appeal to the library director, the person files a formal challenge that eventually ends up on the library board's agenda.

When this kind of situation develops, a library director should make no bones about the fact that what's being confronted is an attempt to censor the library's collection. Don't try to clothe the issue in less pejorative terms. Regardless of how "nice" or "flaky" or "religious" the people making the challenge may be, the issue is censorship, and you must call it that. This is a battle that also is probably going to be fought in the pages of the local newspaper, so it is crucial that the library and its governing authority be proactive, not reactive, to the situation.

Among the very first things a director should do is to notify the intellectual freedom committee of the state library association and the American Library Association Office of Intellectual Freedom (which has an on-line form for doing so). The reason is the light these groups may be able to shed on the organization (if there is one) mounting the challenge—what their past practice as been, the reputation of their attorneys, their success rate, comparable cases, and the like. It is a tried and true rule of conflict: The more you know about your opponent, the better off you will be.

It is also smart to do two other things *immediately*. First, inform the staff of the pending censorship attempt, and what is being done about it. Do it by e-mail, memo, or best, by meeting, so that everyone has a chance to ask questions, and rehearse responses to the public. Circulate the case file, so staff can read the selection librarian's response to the initial complaint. Remind staff not to get trapped into discussions of the book itself. The issue is the library's obligation to provide material representing all viewpoints.

Second, "refresh" the library governing authority, and especially the Chair, on the principles of the *Library Bill of Rights* and its relevant Interpretations. Give them new copies. The board probably adopted this document years ago. Unless it has had a recent discussion of it, the members (and they may be new members) are not likely to be up-to-date on its implications. Here's another tried and true rule of conflict: *Never* let a politician be surprised by a question from the press. If the official doesn't know what the reporter is talking about, and embarrasses himself by saying the first thing that pops into his head (for example, "Gosh, we've got a book about *that*?") guess whose fault it will be?

Finally, building coalitions for intellectual freedom in advance is always good strategy. If you haven't had a chance to do that formally, at least prepare yourself by listing the groups in town who you are pretty sure you can call on in an emergency. Not the least of these will be your own Library Friends group, who are as likely to be as well prepared as anyone to mount a quick information mobilization on the library's behalf. And every library can count on the local chapter of the American Civil Liberties Union for support. Virtually any other group in your community, from businesswomen's service organizations to the Central Labor Council, can be turned into allies if they are forcefully reminded that censorship of free speech at the library is the beginning of censorship of everyone's free speech.

Wading Ashore Always Looks Good

Working with the Chair of the board, you should call in every chit you ever had with the working press, starting at the top with the local paper's editorial board, and going down through the ranks of individual reporters. Call them up, and ask for a meeting or an interview. Try to get them started into the issue from the standpoint that censorship at the library is the beginning of censorship of everyone's free speech, including the newspaper's.

In talking with reporters, stick to your basic points: libraries must provide material representing all viewpoints—this conflict is *not* about whether homosexuality is good or evil, it is about the right of the people to access to information in their public library. Avoid (if you can) castigating the person or group bringing the complaint, or impugning their motives. Take the high moral and political ground, and don't let any challenger take it away from you: free speech, the First Amendment to the U.S. Constitution, freedom of thought as the American way, "In this country we are not afraid of ideas, but we are afraid of ignorance," and so forth.

Never hesitate to repeat what you have just said, no matter what you are asked—professional politicians do it all the time. Take a minute to think before you answer a question. Control the interview with silence when you aren't ready to talk, or if you don't want to answer. An old reporter's trick is to sit quietly, looking expectant, and wait for you to get nervous and start filling the silence with talk. Turn the tables. Make the reporter ask the questions.

Radio talk and interview shows are very popular media in most communities, so try to get on as many of these as you can. But they do present special problems. Dead air time, i.e., silence, is the cardinal sin on the radio. Sometimes the interviewer will be so antsy that if you take a breath before you answer, he or she will jump in with another question. If you don't think you can be fluent on the radio (that is, talk while you are still thinking up an answer) find someone who can be. The most important thing is to *sound* competent, confident, and assured, as well as warm, friendly, and not threatening. Try pretending that the interviewer is your favorite aunt.

Local television is also problematic, primarily because the news shows deal in 20 second sound bites. This forces the reporters to talk in clichés, and gives you only a tiny moment to get across your message. One on-camera trick is to ignore the reporter's question, and say what you want using your own clichés. It doesn't matter, because the reporter is going to edit the story anyway; your object is to give her or him footage of you saying that the conflict is about the right of the people to access to information. Off camera you can explain the details to the reporter.

The typical television reporter is going to want to wave around a copy of *Daddy's Roommate* and lead with a sentence such as, "Should gay books be allowed in the children's room at the public library? The Pure at Heart Organization says No. They are challenging a book called...."

To a reporter, the most important part of the story is that a group has challenged a specific book. The reporter is going to focus on the group and what it says, unless you can find a means for taking the attention away from them. Try something visual, like a stack of all the books that have ever been banned, beginning with the classics. Talk about Nazis burning books in Germany. Use short sentences, but the most dramatic words you can think of. And don't worry about your hair: Nearly everyone looks awful on television.

One of my favorite quotes about an actual challenge to *Daddy's Roommate* came from a city councilman in Goldsboro, North Carolina. He was also a member of the library board. He told an Associated Press reporter: "If that would be the worst thing we've got in this town, I'd be tickled to death. I have

12 grandchildren and I don't think their reading it would have any effect on them. People ought to be educated as to what is going on is this world."[6] The Library Board in Goldsboro voted 7 to 2 to keep the book in the juvenile social issues area of the collection.

Alas, however, that reasonably satisfactory outcome was not so easily repeated in other communities where this book and others in the same series have been targeted for removal. Other targets of recent challenges have been *Roll of Thunder, Hear My Cry*, Mildred D. Taylor's wonderful book about an African-American family in the South, and the usual author suspects such as Mark Twain, J. D. Salinger, and John Steinbeck. Author Judy Blume, who has been censored quite few times herself, says on her Web site:

> But it not just the books under fire now that worry me. It is the books that will never be written. The books that will never be read. And all due to the fear of censorship. As always, young readers will be the real losers."[7]

How right she is.

Ten Minutes a Week for Training

Here are some questions from library users that can be used for role playing practice by the staff.

1. I certainly think you should have a complete children's collection, but I worry. How do I know what my child is reading?

2. Why does the library keep copies of a book like *Mein Kampf*?

3. Have you ever read *The Color Purple*? The movie may have been great, but the book is disgusting.

4. I really don't think you should let young people read novels like this one; it's about suicide.

5. Why doesn't the library put labels on the videos so we know which ones are bad?

6. So who decides what books the library is going to have? You just get 'em from the publishers' stock lists, am I right?

7. How can the library have something like *The Anarchist Cookbook* on the shelves when we are under constant threat from terrorists?

Chapter 7

E-Mail, Chat Rooms, and Websites: Internet Use in the Library

We were totally unprepared for reality. Our naïve expectation was that people would use the Internet to study history, learn about medical conditions, track stock quotes, do research for college papers and read their hometown newspapers. Kids would be working on school projects. Voters would seek candidate records to prepare for the next election.
—Wendy Adamson, "Sex in the City: What Happened at the Minneapolis Public Library," *Off Our Backs*, September-October 2002[1]

This rather wistful comment is from an article Adamson wrote describing why some members of the Minneapolis Public Library staff decided to go to court, claiming that public use of the Internet was sexually harassing to the library workers. It summarizes what all but the most cynically prescient among us believed would be the case back in 1997 or 1998 as we began making free access to the Internet widely available to the library public.

Instead, we have found ourselves forced to make decisions about e-mail use, time limits, parental permission for children's access, graphic sex sites, and whether to install blocking software. Our staffs have claimed that they are forced into the role of police people. We have fielded complaints from users who want chairs with better lower back support, people who wonder why we don't offer free word processing, and others who complain when we do. We have had to develop procedures for handling visitors to town who want to use our terminals to e-mail home. And many of us have been frustrated to find that we have neither the time nor the resources to train the public in the effective use of this fantastic information resource.

This chapter does not attempt to be a thorough examination of all the legal and other issues that surround public library Internet use. It tries, instead, to suggest some ways to organize the library's response to the challenges raised by these access issues. It is unabashedly opinionated: I do not believe in blocking software, and I *do* believe in enforcing rules preventing adults from accessing obscenity. The procedures I suggest have worked for my library, and adapted to local conditions, also work in many others.

Library literature these days is full of material on all the issues surrounding Internet use. The two best, which I strongly recommend that people read, are *Managing the Internet Controversy*[2] and that old standby for all of us, the *Intellectual Freedom Manual*.[3] I often find collections of essays too "on the one hand this, on the other hand that," but *Managing the Internet Controversy* has brought together a series of very thoughtful articles that nobody should miss. See especially Susan Fuller's essay called "Ethics and the Internet" about the struggles local elected officials had in coping with the filtering issue, and Ann K. Symons' piece, "Working with Parents to Manage Internet Controversy."

Time and Access Issues

Let's start with the nitty-gritty time and access issues, and confront content rules later.

About five minutes (well, all right, it was a month) after my library began offering Internet access, we knew we had a tiger on our hands, and grabbing the tail was going to be a feat. We had people lined up at the door in the morning who would rush in, establish themselves at the terminals, and all but set up housekeeping for the day. They were not even dissuaded by the uncomfortable stools we provided for terminal use.

Our tentative efforts to establish informal time limits ("Let's be fair to everyone here") put the staff in the policing role that no one wanted. Reference services at the Central Library were quickly falling by the wayside as staff dealt with Internet access problems and at the smaller branches service demands were driving the public desk staffs nuts. Even after we imposed sign-up sheets and serious time limits, we discovered that users were moving from branch to branch to give themselves all-day access.

Our automation staff came to the rescue. They researched and found a software program (Cybraryn, but there are several others available) that put us back in control. Users must now have a borrower card to use the Internet, they sign up for a time certain that day, and they are limited to one hour's use per day anywhere in the Library System. No more moving from the Central Branch to Live Oak to Aptos. Patrons are warned five minutes before their time is up, and automatically shut down when it is. The desk staff is also able to shut down a specific terminal if a patron is abusing the rules.

Visitors to Santa Cruz (which is a beach resort and university town, so this is a serious issue) must come to the desk, show a photo ID or a passport, and be officially logged on as a temporary borrower. Staff regards this as an annoyance, but knows there isn't really a viable alternative short of limiting use to Santa Cruz County residents only. And no town reliant on tourist dollars would do that. The whole thing came home to me clearly one afternoon last summer, as I was walking down our main street with a colleague. Two backpack-wearing youngsters stopped us and said, "Can you tell us where the public library is?"

Was it my sensible shoes that tipped them off to the fact that I would know? "Two blocks over and one down," I said.

"Great. Gotta e-mail home."

But in the fall of 2003, confronting a serious budget shortfall, we realized that we were not obligated to provide free Internet access to people without library cards. Since we issue borrower cards to virtually any state resident who has the right identification (including homeless people based at the local shelter), why shouldn't we charge people who only want to use the Internet $5 an hour for the service? The commercial establishments in town charge $6 to $12 for access, so the public library is still a good deal. Of course, we don't sell lattes.

The software control system has been working well since its inception. There is the occasional shocked outrage when a computer cuts someone off ("I'm sorry, sir. You did get a five minute warning"), but generally people understand. The evidence of high demand is obvious: every terminal is booked in every time slot at Central and the other larger branches.

Problems do occur at smaller sites, where a user being bounced off the terminal may notice that there are one or two other empty ones. "Why can't I keep working?" the user will ask. "There isn't anyone else here who wants to use it." "We need to keep terminals available for people who are just coming in," the staff explains. And we try to train workers to use our own common sense rule: if it is pouring with rain and a slow day anyway, for goodness sake give the user another hour if he or she wants it.

Protecting User Privacy

There are two issues here: physical siting of the internet terminals, and record keeping. Despite a boom in library building over the last five years, I'm afraid the truth is that most of us occupy buildings designed and furnished long before the Internet became part of our daily lives. Having moved out the card catalogs, most of us have our Internet access computers lined up shoulder to shoulder down the center of the library's main floor. Siting the terminals so that a user can view information without the danger of someone else seeing what he or she is doing is a practical impossibility. There are a few mitigations, but none of them work especially well. Filters can be installed on the screens, although these are rather expensive. Or wing-like screens can be affixed to the sides of the terminals. Carrels with sides offer the most privacy, but also take up the most space. Frankly, I think it is sensible to argue that using the Internet in a public space like the library means that the user cannot expect to have the privacy he or she would have at home.

A user *can* expect that her use of the library's Internet service is confidential information, as is data about the sites she accessed. Just as we hold materials checkout information confidential, so patron Internet use should be too. Some libraries are lucky enough to have computer on-line booking systems that control the data, and purge use records on a daily basis. Others have manual sign-up sheets that must be shredded at the close of business each day. The point is that a Library Internet Use Policy should contain a statement about user privacy, and the staff should have procedures in place to ensure that it is implemented.

User Problems: Access for Children

The issue here, of course, is the fear that children will access inappropriate materials, which can range from straight-out pornography to a health information web site that a child's parents may view as wrong or too sophisticated for the child. The option of installing blocking software is discussed later in this Chapter.

The response of public librarians to children's use seems to fall in two categories: those who focus on taking strong protective measures, and those who concern themselves more with encouraging parent responsibility. The two strategies are not mutually exclusive, but they do tend to reflect different philosophical approaches.

Tools for strong protective measures include installing blocking software (see below), close monitoring of child use, and requiring parental permission before a child can use the library computers that offer Internet access. The permissions are written, and are often keyed into a child's borrower card so that access can be denied or granted easily. These rules require a lot of effort on the part of staff, who may or may not feel that their communities demand this kind of oversight.

The other school of thought holds that parents are responsible for what their children read and view, that the library is not *in loco parentis*, and the

Internet is a format for information like any other. Therefore, the library staff's efforts should be focused on teaching parents and kids how to use the resource: coaching one-on-one, conducting training workshops, developing find-it tools, and the like. Carolyn Noah's article, "Steering Kids to Solo Navigation: Implementing Internet Service for Young People" in *Managing the Internet Controversy* offers some excellent help on doing this, including descriptions of successful library projects.[4]

Any library will certainly want to promulgate rules against children viewing obscenity, which is against the law. Enforcing the rules requires clear sight lines to the Internet computers, constant vigilance during the after-school hours, and a feel for which pre-teen and teenage boys are looking for trouble and need special attention. Our experience has been that boys in this category are mostly testing us, and that a strong initial response solves the problem.

Content Problems: E-mail, Chat Rooms, and Games

Frankly, I used to see e-mail as a tool like the telephone. We don't provide free phone access to the public, so why do we provide free e-mail? But I was dissuaded from this curmudgeonly position when I found myself more and more often using e-mail to acquire information. However, sorting out what's a message to somebody's Mom ("Having a wonderful time; send money") and access to the electronic newsletter of an organization to which a user belongs is not a job a library worker has the time to do. So, with terminal use time limits in place, the sensible rule seems to be allowing e-mail use. Some libraries don't, however. See the sample Internet Policies on the ALA Office of Intellectual Freedom Web site.

Chat rooms present serious security problems for kids and adults with little or no sophistication. They can get seduced into giving their names and addresses to people they don't know. It is crucial that libraries make Chat room behavior and safety a part of Internet instruction. Another problem with Chat rooms is that adults can get so absorbed in a discussion that they lose track of the time and then are indignant when the buzzer (as it were) goes off. "But I haven't sent my e-mail yet," they say plaintively to the staff. Sorry, too bad. Others are waiting. Again, some libraries do not allow this use at all.

I wish I felt really comfortable justifying use of the public Internet access terminals for games. However, as any youth services librarian will be quick to point out, games are educational, they promote eye-hand coordination, they convey information in an interactive way, and heaven knows what other useful things. I would hate to think that the library was valued for the Internet access it provides to *3D Pinball*, but I myself have crossed the country by covered wagon playing *Oregon Trail* and can attest to the concrete value of the experience. Again, having a system of time limits is the key to making this work.

Content Problems: Pornography

Okay, now we get to the exciting and truly difficult stuff: The astonishing array of sexually explicit sites on the Internet that can offend adult library users and staff, and if they depict children, are patently illegal. One of the problems here is the language we use to talk about it. "Pornography," except as it relates to children, is not a legal term. Neither are "soft porn," "hard porn," or "erotica." Even the term "sexually explicit" doesn't work as a descriptor because it encompasses medical sites about, for example, prostate cancer, as well as those meant to provoke sexual arousal.

I suspect that most people believe they know what any of these things are and can recognize them when they see them. The problem, of course, is the difference between Mrs. Jones' conviction that full frontal nudity in any form is erotica, and Mrs. Smith's belief that the same is actually great art.

This would not be nearly such a problem were it not for the public nature of Internet use in libraries. About the only way we could completely guarantee privacy would be to set up special booths for Internet use. Few libraries have the space for that, although there was a widespread rumor a couple of years ago that the San Francisco Public Library had a special room at Main for viewing porn. Not true, said the Director, and pointed me to the Internet Use Policy on the San Francisco Website.

"We have pc's scattered throughout Main and some are in fairly private locations," Director Susan Hildreth said. "If people ask for a private location to look at health or other material for which they want privacy, we direct them there. I do think folks have figured out where these locations are and try to get to them, but our online booking system does not allow users to ask for specific pc's."[5]

The problem for the library boils down to forcing patrons to distinguish between what is appropriate viewing in the privacy of one's home (anything they want), and what can be viewed in the library public space. The library's task is to set up rules that satisfy the local community's sense of what they think they have a right *not to be exposed to* at the same time that it tries to protect an individual's right to information.

The American Library Association's Intellectual Freedom Committee has done wonderful work sorting out the issues involved here. The following lengthy quote is from "Guidelines and Considerations in Developing a Public Library Internet Use Policy" in the *Intellectual Freedom Manual*.

Obscenity and child pornography are illegal. Federal and state statutes, the latter varying slightly depending on the jurisdiction, proscribe such materials. The U.S. Supreme Court has settled most questions about what obscenity and child pornography statutes are constitutionally sound.

According to the Court:

Obscenity must be determined using a three-part test. To be obscene, (1) the average person, applying contemporary community standards, must find that the work, taken as whole, appeals to prurient interests; (2) the work must depict or describe, in a patently offensive way, sexual conduct as specified in the applicable statutes; and (3) the work, taken as a whole, must lack serious literary, artistic, political, or scientific value.

Child pornography may be determined using a slightly less rigorous test. To be child pornography, the work must involve depictions of sexual conduct specified in the applicable statutes and use images of children below a specified age.

Many states and some localities have "harmful to minors" laws. These laws regulate free speech with respect to minors, typically forbidding the display or dissemination of certain sexually explicit materials to children, as further specified in the laws.

According to the Supreme Court:

Materials harmful to minors include descriptions or representations of nudity, sexual conduct, or sexual excitement that appeal to prurient, shameful, or morbid interest of minors; are patently offensive to prevailing standards in the adult community as a whole with respect to what is suitable material for minors; and lack serious literary, artistic, political, or scientific value for minors.[6]

Anybody reading this can see where the problem starts, and it isn't with child pornography. The problem is making a rule forbidding adults to access Internet sites that meet the community definition of pornography, and then being forced by a litigious user to decide what material meets the obscenity definition and what has literary, artistic, political, or social value. Only the courts can do that, not working librarians.

However, the courts have *also* ruled that a public library is a limited public forum that may set rules for use. As Chapter 1 of this book explains, the rules must meet certain criteria: they must be narrowly tailored to the purpose of the institution and designed to protect a significant government interest. If they deny access they must leave open some alternative channel for receiving the information. Coupled with local laws and local custom, it seems to me that this offers ample grounds for making rules that forbid adults from viewing at least obscene and possibly pornographic materials on library Internet terminals.

To Block or Not to Block

There is another solution, of course—to install software that filters out the pornographic/obscene/harmful to minors sites. Indeed, the Child Internet

Protection Act (CIPA) requires public libraries that wish to receive E-rate discounts, or Library Services and Technology Act funds for internet access or internet computers, to install blocking software on all their computers.[7] This includes not only the computers adults and children use, but the staff computers as well. The software is a specific technology that blocks or filters Internet access to visual depictions of child pornography, obscenity, and material that is harmful to minors.

The problem with it is that it doesn't work. Study after study has demonstrated[8] that not only are pornographic and obscene Web sites still accessible when filters are in place, but that sites providing access to scientific, consumer, and even political information are also blocked. Thus both library users and staff are denied access to information they need—a clear infringement of First Amendment rights. There may well be instances in which blocking software is an appropriate means for controlling children's access to the Internet—but as a panacea for protecting the adult information-seeking public from viewing of pornography or obscenity (either by accident or design), the software does not work.

During 2003–04 public libraries across the country will make decisions about whether they choose to comply with CIPA, as the Court requires, or give up their eligibility for certain grant funds. It may well be, however, that more litigation will further complicate and/or confuse the issue. The Supreme Court's remedy for the First Amendment denial was to specify that the blocking software must be turned off whenever an adult patron requests it. The Justices seemed to be under the impression that blocking software works like a light switch—on and off, at any terminal.

This just isn't true. Any automation system operating via networked servers will require an exceedingly cumbersome set of procedures to un-block, plus (and here's the nightmare) tech staff at every site standing ready to implement them.

Internet Use Policy Guidelines

The ALA Intellectual Freedom Committee advises public libraries to adopt a comprehensive, written Internet use policy that should:

> Set forth reasonable time, place, and manner restrictions;
>
> Expressly prohibit any use of library equipment to access material that is obscene, child pornography, or "harmful to minors" (consistent with any applicable state or local law);
>
> Provide for the privacy of users with respect to public terminals; and
>
> Protect the confidentiality of records, electronic or otherwise, that identify individual users and link them to search strategies, sites accessed, or other specific data about the information they retrieved or sought to retrieve.[9]

The Committee also advises that the library communicate its Internet use rules to all library users (including parents), that it post notices at all Internet-access computers about the rules, offer well-publicized training programs, and recommend Internet sites, especially to youngsters and their parents. This is all excellent advice.

The ALA Office of Intellectual Freedom Web page offers access to a variety of policy and guidelines documents surrounding the Internet issue. It also provides six sample policies from libraries across the country. The one thing that isn't there is the actual wording for the signs that libraries should post. So how about the following?

> *Library equipment may not be used to access pornography, material that is obscene or is harmful to minors, or other illegal activity, such as hacking. Library users who do so will be required to stop immediately. Repeated offenses will result in permanent denial of access to the Internet at the library.*

Ten Minutes a Week for Training

Here are some problem situation scenarios staff might discuss in the context of your library's Internet use policy. Three relate to difficult encounters with patrons, and the fourth is meant as a reminder that the Internet is not the be-all and end-all of our existence.

1. An eleven year old girl, using the Internet in the Children's Room, enters the term "kittens" to get information on how to care for her new tabby. Instead, a site called Sex Kittens for You comes up, scaring the daylights out of her. The staff shows her how to get out of the site, of course, and she ends up telling her dad about the experience. He comes to the Youth Services Desk and wants to know why the Library isn't protecting his daughter form obscenity and material harmful to minors.

2. The Director was making a report to the Board about Internet use in the library, how demand was rising, how the software limiting time of use seemed to be working, and how the staff was starting a new "Saturday Morning at the Library" training hour for users. "I was in using the Internet last week," said one trustee. "I noticed that the person next to me seemed to be spending his whole time in one of those Chat Rooms talking about baseball, for heaven's sake. I don't understand why you let people do that. Shouldn't we be limiting Internet use to people doing *real* research instead of these folks who just want to talk?"

3. "Oh no!" says the man using one of the Internet workstations. "I don't want this! How do I stop this damn thing?" It turns out he has accessed a sex

site, and lewd pictures are popping up on the screen. As people around him
glare, the staff person on duty attempts to close the site, and ends up having to turn off the terminal. The patron is mightily embarrassed. The situation isn't helped by a passing user, who takes the opportunity to point out
in a loud voice that if the library installed blocking software this kind of thing
would not be a problem. How should the staff person respond?

4. "I know this is on the Web," says the patron at the Reference Desk. "I just
can't find it." What he wants are the addresses of the Bureaus of Prisons in
four Western states. "No problem," says the Reference Librarian. "Let's
look at the California Bureau of Prisons Web site, because I know they have
addresses for agencies in other states." As soon as he gets the California
Bureau up on the screen he remembers what an impenetrable mess this site
is. And he also remembers that on a shelf not six feet away is a hard copy
directory of all prisons and prison bureaus in the United States. He gives
the information to the patron, and files the incident away as an example of
why the Internet is not always the best source of information. Can the staff
think of other examples?

Part III
Practical Advice

Chapter 8

Securing Our Buildings

Did you know that among experienced library vandals a popular method for removing pages from books and periodicals involves wet thread? You moisten the thread with spit and then lay it along the binding seam of the page you want. You close the book or magazine, hold the thread at one end, pull it from the other, and bingo! out comes the page.

This is a technique one of the experts described at an Ameican Library Association Annual Conference program on building security, and his podium colleagues agreed with him. So of course I went home and tried it. I couldn't make it work, with either a paperback or an old *New Yorker*. I even used two different kinds of thread. Could it be that my saliva is not acidic enough? Or that I don't have the right wrist action? Whatever the case, as an observer pointed out (he couldn't get it to work either), if you wanted to mutilate magazines, wouldn't it be easier to use one of those little retractable single-blade razors encased in plastic, which are actually *meant* to be used for newspaper clipping? They are small enough to hide in the palm of the hand, and you don't have to worry about drooling.

The issue of materials mutilation came up at the ALA program in the context of what librarians should be looking for as they observe the users in their buildings. See someone with unexplained thread sticking out of his/her pocket (or mouth)? Watch out, because he/she could be after the new SUV ratings in *Consumer Reports*.

This chapter is about what *else* librarians should be looking for—not just suspicious actions by patrons, but the physical arrangements inside our buildings that either can deter problem behavior or make it easier. The focus mainly is on the small and middle size libraries that do not have security forces of their own, and which constitute the majority of all public libraries in the nation. Although much of the specific advice comes from the security professionals, I have tried to collect guidelines, procedures, and ideas that can be implemented by library staffs working only with their local police forces.[1]

With regard to physical arrangements, there are many of us around the country saddled with inappropriate buildings—or those ironies of modern design—the prize-winning structure that looks so wonderful in the four color spreads of *Architectural Record*, but turns out to be a security nightmare to work in. Even in the worst buildings, however, there are some ameliorative steps that can be taken. And on this score, the local police can often be helpful.

Working with the Police

Librarians want two things from the police: trust that when library staff calls, the cops will believe them, and quick response time. Achieving those objectives requires building a collegial relationship in which both the library staff and the police understand each other's work environment. It was suggested in Chapter 4 that this means bridging the gap between library staff values and those of the police.

One way to do this is for the library director to ask the chief of police to assist in conducting a security assessment of the library building. Even if the library is not able (or is unwilling) to take all the advice given, at least the police officers will develop some understanding of how the library works and why it does what it does.

It is also remarkable what cops can think up if they are invited to be part of the prevention process, rather than merely the cleaner-uppers at the end.

For example, a few years ago we were having trouble with "sleepovers" at the downtown branch of the Santa Cruz library. Street people (we assumed) would elude the security sweep conducted by the staff at closing time, and spend the night in the building. We didn't have enough money to hire a night guard, and the Police Department was stretched too thin to provide more than semi-regular checkups of the building exterior.

One day, genius struck our police chief.

"Listen," he said on the phone. "You can help me solve a problem, and I think I've got a solution for you, too. I've got these canine units? Well, they have to be trained all the time. How would you feel about my cops using the library as a training site? We'd bring in the dogs and their officers, say, three nights a week, and do an exercise with them in your building. What time does your computer operator come on?"

"About 5 A.M.," I said.

"Perfect," said the chief. "We'd be in and out between midnight and 4 A.M. We've got warning decals you could put on the doors. What do you think?"

"Perfect," I said. And we have never had another sleep-over problem. When the computer operator changed her hours, she got introduced to the canine units, and they are all the best of friends. She says the dogs are very sweet when they know you. You can even pet them.

Security Surveys, Part I: Buildings

Every security expert, management consultant, and police officer advises that librarians make security surveys of their building and operations. The survey needs to look at the building in terms of how potential problem behaviors (flashing, purse snatching, vandalism and the like) are made easier by the physical arrangement. A library also needs to assess what its current problem behaviors are, and consider how physical changes and modifications in operations would help.

MICROFORM MACHINES, OPACS AND OTHER EQUIPMENT

The security issue here is vandalism. Microfilm machines and public access catalog terminals need to be located in places where they are visible to the staff. And if that cannot be done in all cases, at least put them in places where other members of the public can see them. Most people are willing to report abuse when they see it, even if they don't find themselves able to intervene personally

STACK AREAS

Stacks are the great security bane of all libraries. It is a pity we need them to shelve the books, because they offer so much potential for criminal use. They are tall for easy hiding behind, fixed in place so that they can't be moved without major money and effort, there are long aisles between them that require exits at *both* ends, and their lighting must run the same way they do if the contents of the shelves is to be seen. This latter point is particularly annoying, because it reduces flexibility in solving security problems: one starts out to turn the stacks to run at a better angle for sight lines from the Circulation Desk, only to realize that every single ceiling fixture will also have to be moved. That will be another $2,000 please.

A favorite ploy of architects, and a real temptation for librarians too, is to use the wall-like stacks to create nifty little nooks and crannies in which to shelve the odd subject collection (genealogy, historic cookbooks, and the like). But these can create terrible security problems. If special small areas cannot be seen by the staff, and aren't well lit, they can easily become havens for, even invitations to, problem behavior.

Many small and mid-sized libraries are arranged so that the stacks radiate out from a central area. Space is preserved at the far ends for access, and the end passage is often left wide enough for study carrels or tables. This is not a good idea. All sitting/reading/study space in a library should have good sight lines to the exit doors for their users and be reasonably easy to see by staff. Even though it makes for a noisier environment, it is best to keep the tables and other sitting areas out in the main area if at all possible.

RESTROOMS

These are another bane, and again, it is a great pity that libraries are public facilities, and therefore need (and are often required) to offer restrooms to users. Restroom security problems are a little easier to reduce than those of book stacks, however. The object is to ensure that the facilities are available for secure, unharassed use by those who need them.

One relatively inexpensive option is to install devices that keep the restroom lights on at all times. With such a system, lights must be turned off at a master control, thereby preventing (for instance) a man with criminal intent from reaching around the women's room door, flicking off the lights, and coming in. Or a jokey kid doing the same thing. This kind of device can be installed in any library area—a back hall, the lobby leading to the meeting room, that cul-de-sac that no one knows why was in the design plan—where guaranteed lighting would be a good idea.

Security consultants sometimes also recommend installing emergency telephones in restrooms and other isolated areas. This sounds like asking for trouble to me, but a library might investigate it if it has the money (lots) and thinks it would solve a local problem.

Restrooms located away from the beaten path—down a long hall or in the basement—can be a nightmare. Even if locked, protecting children going to and from them is very hard. The best solution is to move them. If that can't be done, then try installing hallway-reflecting mirrors, to keep some tabs on what is going on. Another solution is video surveillance, or even *fake* video surveillance. Apparently it is not difficult to purchase or rig up the kind of cameras that *look* like they are photographing activities in a certain area, when in fact they are not. Of course, standard sensibilities require that these cameras not be in positions to intrude on users' private activities, so this is not a panacea. But the police department can give you advice on a security firm that handles this kind of equipment.

The best way to promote restroom security is to keep the facilities locked. This is an option that the desk staff may hate, since it creates key-handing-out and time-monitoring work for them, and some of the public won't like it much either. On the other hand, it is one of the only ways to prevent misuse and abuse of restrooms. Explained in these terms, the staff and public alike have a basis for understanding and agreement. Separate restrooms for children, limited exclusively to their use, and again controlled by keys, offer the best restroom security protection against child molesters. Locking the restrooms also helps cut down on the pilfering of toilet paper and paper towels, because the staff can require that totes, backpacks, etc.—if allowed in the first place (and perhaps they shouldn't be)—be left at the desk in exchange for the key.

Finally, if the library building is an old one, or is located in shopping center or other non-traditional space, check all the doors, and especially those to the restrooms. Are the key slots of the locks on the correct side? Is there a button lock on the inside of a door where you don't want one (for example, the children's restroom?) Before you laugh, think how infuriated (and frightened) you would be if you got locked in a hallway that you couldn't exit. This happened at the Boston Public Library a few years ago, and the trapped woman died.

LIBRARY ENTRANCES AND EXITS

Adequate lighting is one of the two security issues here. A conscientious librarian will walk in and out of the building at night, experimenting with various routes to the bus stop, the parking lot, or a major cross street. Is there enough ambient light so that a user of any age feels comfortable walking to his/her car? Is there also adequate light on the disabled access ramp? Can the sidewalk be seen well enough to ensure that most patrons won't trip on hazards such as broken concrete?

Every library, no matter how small, needs at least two entrances, so that the building can be evacuated safely in case of fire or earthquake. The second entrance can have an alarm device on it to ensure that is only used in emergencies. The locksmith can be asked to put a fifteen or twenty second time delay on the lock. This will help the staff get there in time to catch a thief stealing books (or at least see which way s/he is heading).

Staff entrances present an additional group of problems. First there is the great tendency to leave them unlocked. This is especially true if not every staff person (or volunteer) has a key. If only library personnel used the back door, this wouldn't be a problem. But every delivery person, citizen wanting to donate books, patron off the street looking for a short cut, *and the odd wallet thief*, also want to use the staff entrance. Keep it locked. Insist that the staff and other legitimate users ring the bell if they don't have a key.

Another reason why staff entrance security is important is because so many of these doors are located at the back of the technical services area. This gives any unsupervised delivery person, not to mention that woman the staff thought was a volunteer but doesn't seem to be around anymore, easy access to a very precious commodity: the books, CDs, and videos lined up on the shelves waiting for processing. Naked of any property markings, they are ripe for the picking by a quick-fingered thief.

Security experts advise, by the way, that libraries look carefully at their processing procedures: get new items into the pipeline as fast as possible, with property stamping an early step. This doesn't necessarily cut down on pilfering for personal use, but it does help prevent organized conspiracies to steal from the library and resell to used bookstores or on the streets. Another good idea is to move the shelves where the just-unpacked books are kept out of the main traffic stream.

KEYS

Theoretically, only staff (never volunteers, trustees, or members of the Library Friends group) should have exterior keys to the building. This is a hard rule to enforce, however, if only for convenience reasons. Who on a small staff really wants to be the one to get out of bed on Sunday morning and truck down to the library to let in the Friends President, who left something behind when she was here yesterday for the book sale.

If tight control of who gets keys can't be enforced, at least organize the key program carefully. Make sure that the bare minimum number of people have master keys that open every lock. The rest should get separate keys for each space. Never issue a key without writing it down on a master list, and do the same when one is loaned. Make *getting keys back* a check off item when an employee leaves, and make turning in keys a condition of getting her/his last paycheck. If payroll checks are issued from a separate city office, this will require coordination, but that shouldn't be hard: finance people are notoriously security conscious.

The key issue is further complicated by the question of what happens when a person leaves the library's employment. This is especially troublesome if the person departs under less than pleasant circumstances. Shouldn't all the locks for which the person had a key be changed? That can get mighty expensive mighty fast. One solution for the exterior entrance is to install push button or key card devices. A code is set for the push button (the least expensive have six buttons and use four digit codes) and then whenever somebody leaves you change the code. This of course means that everyone must be notified and must memorize the new code. And if a lot of people work in the building the security of this device is substantially diminished.

Key cards turn out to be a better, and probably in the long run a cheaper solution. The card activates the un-locking device when waved in front of it. Cards come in credit-card size, or for more money, much more popular fobs that fit on key chains. The great advantage is that instead of having to change the code when a person leaves, you simply remove the person from the authorized users on the system, thereby deactivating their key card.

Staff Nametags

Maybe if we called nametags "security tags" there wouldn't be such fuss from staff about wearing them. The point of a tag is to identify who is an employee or person with a valid reason for being in the staff areas of the library, and who isn't. If only ten people work in the building, security tags aren't necessary because everyone knows everyone else.

Even small libraries, however, may have a constantly changing group of student pages, who turn up for work at odd hours looking like typical high school or college kids (or worse). It is impossible for anyone but their supervisor to keep track of who they are. Require them to wear buttons which say LIBRARY PAGE. Get comparable buttons for volunteers and Friends of the Library. Using buttons (which are cheap) is also good public relations: It identifies people on the floor who might be able to answer a directional question, and it advertises the volunteer program and the Friends organization.

As for staff security tags, the principal objection to them seems to be that displaying the employee's first and last name is a security violation in itself. Oh come. The name part of a permanent tag can go on the back side. The point is to identify who is a legitimate staff member at the library.

Signage

Security experts set great store by having readable, well-lit signs. There are two reasons. The first is that fire and other regulations require that exits on every floor be clearly identified. The second is the overall ambience of the library: If the directional and location signs are accurate and make sense, the image of an orderly institution in which appropriate behavior is expected is enhanced.

Frank DeRosa, the Director of Facilities Management and Risk Control at the Brooklyn Public Library (and the man who told the ALA audience about usefulness of wet thread) is also a strong advocate of posted rules signs. He says a common response from a library user who is asked to stop doing something is "Show me where it sez...." In California, this would be "Hey, man, like show me where it says...." Pointing out the sign which says no smoking or whatever is a good response. On the second request to cease and desist, the Brooklyn Public Library security staff give the perpetrator a 5" by 7" handbill which lists the behavior rules. This sounds like a good idea for any size library.

Security Surveys, Part II: Assessing Current Problems

The second part of a security survey of the library is a look at current problems. What are the typical broken rules, criminal acts, or behaviors the library is experiencing. A rash of flasher incidents? A series of stolen wallet reports? As one security expert put it, assessing security problems is largely a matter of asking the right questions. The old journalism mnemonic is useful here. Look for the five Ws: Who, What, When, Where, and Why, although not necessarily in that order. And the answers to these questions should provide clues for how operations or furniture arrangements or whatever might be adjusted.

For example, if theft of patron possessions is a mounting problem, perhaps the library should think about increasing the number of "don't leave your backpack or purse unattended" signs. Or taping small cards with the same message to every table and study carrel. If the library believes that men are hanging about in the children's room for unacceptable reasons, it should look at taking out the lounge chairs, even if this makes it more difficult for parents to read comfortably to their children. Are many of the problems occurring at one time period each day (when school dismisses, before the soup kitchen opens, etc.)? What about deploying as many pages as possible during those hours, so there is a big staff presence on the floor?

Hearsay and anecdotal descriptions at staff meetings are not enough to determine what a library's security problems are. Documentation is needed, and to document such things a library needs a form. Even the staff at a tiny one-room facility in the middle of the desert needs to write down, clearly and coherently, what happened when that green convertible screeched to a halt in front of the building, Thelma and Louise jumped out and rushed through the door, making off with the week's accumulated overdue fine money. Actually, it was only $5.35, so they won't get far, but still....

Seriously. Appendix C includes a sample Incident Report Form. Staff should be trained to use these whenever anything out of the ordinary occurs. Among other reasons, the forms are a means for laying a good paper trail. And the library will need one if it decides to secure a no trespassing order against a patron. Branch managers will find that the forms are a useful way of keeping central administration aware of how tough things are on the front lines, and the administration can use them to document emerging problems and budget requests.

Planning a New Building

All of the rules regarding security evaluations in an existing building should be adapted in planning a new one. The magic of a new facility is that—potentially at least—the library gets to start from scratch, with shelving lined up the right way, adequate lighting, restrooms in visible places, windows in the doors of offices so they can be easily inspected, and even a staff entrance separate from the technical services department.

Actually, it is sometimes very difficult to get these kinds of security protections built into the plans for a new building, especially working with an architect who hasn't designed a library before. Many are the award winning buildings which have impossible sight lines and are filled with obscure corners. It is therefore always smart to get a library building consultant on the project who will look out for the library's security and other interests as the plans and specifications are evaluated. Sad to say, the advice of such a consultant carries more weight than the requests of a working librarian who is saying the same thing, even when what's being asked for is just good common sense (a circulation desk near the front entrance/exit, stairwells which can be inspected easily, regular shapes, and so forth).

Ten Minutes a Week for Training

It is astonishing how difficult it is to get staff, particularly those at the busiest sites, to remember to fill out Incident Reports. Actually, the problem isn't getting them to remember to do it, it is getting them to take the time to do it. To reinforce the consciousness of necessity, a library might devote an occasional training session to a discussion of the form and when and how it is filled out.

Another useful training discussion topic is a review of the month's incidents and how they were handled: this is always good for morale if they were handled well, and teaches a good deal even if they weren't. Ask questions of the people who confront the problems: would moving the furniture fix it? Does the library need a daily walk-through from the police? Suppose we simply closed that restroom off, and made everyone use the facility on the main floor?

Chapter 9

Writing Good Manuals

It occurs to me that there are only two kinds of library staff manuals—the kind people read and/or otherwise use, and the kind they don't. As it happens, I have ample experience with both, and I vastly prefer the first kind. There are few things more satisfying than seeing a manual you've spent days and weeks putting together actually used, and used effectively. On the other hand, how humiliating it is to find one's brilliantly conceived instructional handbook gathering dust on a hidden shelf under the reference desk!

The Santa Cruz Library staff and I spent much of the summer of 1988 putting together comprehensive emergency manuals for each of our library branches. In October, 1989, disaster struck: a major earthquake wreaked substantial havoc throughout this section of California. We had roughly 350,000 books on the floor system-wide, and other major damage, but every branch was evacuated safely, and we opened for service again only six days later. Staff had read the manual and knew what to do. They had inventoried all emergency supplies two weeks before the earthquake, right on the manual's schedule. This meant that every flashlight was where it was supposed to be, and even had a working battery.

On the other hand, I was the lead author of an automation system manual that met a primary need during the first year or so we were on line, but increasingly became less useful. Either the manual was too simple for a staff that became very automation-savvy quite quickly, or the system was too complicated for the kind of information the manual endeavored to convey. Probably it was both. A staff committee wrote the successor manual, which is twice the length of the original—and well over my head with details that only primary users of the system would know. All the circulation staff people think the new version is just great. "You can *find* things in it," they report happily. I try not to be hurt by the implications of this comment.

These two examples lead me to draw some conclusions about what constitutes a good staff manual. The first is that one must be very clear about the purpose such a document is meant to serve, and then design, write, and put it in a form that meets that objective. An Emergency Manual, for example, is supposed to tell the staff exactly what to do when an earthquake hits ("Duck, Cover, and Hold," as we say in California), or how long to keep the library open if the power goes off. The whole point is to give precise information and instructions. What is wanted is a document that can be referred to quickly in, dare I say it, an emergency. Explanations are nice, but not required. And in fact, explication of the whys and wherefores of rabies vaccination can get in the way of the hard information about what to do if a dog bites a patron.

An automation system manual, on the other hand, has a lot more room for explanation, because its primary purpose is as a training and reference tool—staff check it when they can't remember how to do something.

These days libraries are also able to make a basic formatting choice: will the manual be on the staff intranet or published in hardcopy or both? The answer depends on the purpose and the audience for the manual. People disagree with me about this, but I think if you need quick access to the information, you can put it on-line, but you should certainly have it available in hard copy too. It may be easier to update the Emergency Manual on the computer, but the procedures to be followed aren't going to do you any good on-line if the power is down.

If you have a problem situation manual that you want every single staff person to read and understand, do not expect them to sit at a terminal somewhere (assuming they can find an empty one) and absorb the information. Give them a hard copy so they can read it in a comfortable chair in the staff lounge or even at home. Put it on-line too, if you wish. But retain the flexibility of hard copy distribution.

On the other hand, the aforesaid Santa Cruz automation system manual (still called "The Blue Book," its 1985 title) is now resident on the staff intranet, where it can be updated quickly, there are links to other programs, and so forth

Another manual-writing criterion is the intended audience. Obviously, there is a vast difference between what we write about the automation system for the people who must operate it, e.g., the circulation and technical services staff, and what we might put in a training manual for the pages, who don't work the circulation desk, but may be called on to help a confused user at a public access catalog terminal.

There is also a difference in style if we are writing for training, or writing for reference, or writing for both. And this point brings me to the issue of what might constitute a useful manual to help staff handle problem situations in libraries.

Problem Situation Manuals—
Purpose, Style, and Content

In the course of working on this book I have collected several examples of staff problem situation (or "problem patron" or "customer relations") manuals. They seem to fall into two genres: the ones with short and precise instructions for what to do about a specific problem, and those that are longer because they feature more explanation and narrative.

I have also observed that the concise ones have a certain similarity, leading me to believe that either there is a central computer somewhere into which each staff committee assigned to write a manual is secretly plugged, or, the same tattered copy of the Original Problem Patron Manual is being passed from library to library.

Back in 1984, when the Santa Cruz library staff prepared its first manual (called *Problem Patrons: A Coping Manual for Staff*) we cribbed most of it from a comparable document prepared by the Schenectady County (New York) Public Library. Seven years later the hot new manual being described in the press was from a library in Southern California. The new lingo was "customer" rather than "patron," but most of the procedures were straight from Schenectady. And in 1992, when I wrote to a library director in Texas for permission to use a section of her library's manual in Appendix C, she very nicely wrote back to say that in fact the procedure I was interested in had been taken from a manual produced by a library in the Northwest, and perhaps I should go directly to the source. It turned out theirs was based on Schentectedy too.

Clearly, one thing that governs the style of a manual is the experience of the staff. In reviewing the record, I note with some surprise that back in 1984 the Santa Cruz staff committee and I were at pains to provide careful and usually colorless instructions on how to handle things such as "Suspicious Behavior" and "Assault." The Appendix was larded with quotations from the state penal code and instructions and diagrams for self-defense, such as

> Strike, kick, stomp, jab, or poke these vulnerable parts as fast and as hard as you can. If your target is the nose, do not just hit the nose, aim through the nose to the back of the head.

It occurs to me that this was a response provoked by a staff confronting a time of great change: increasing numbers of street people were appearing in the library, many workers were worried for their personal safety, new user groups were making demands for service, the library was automating, and to top it all off, a new director had come to town.

So the staff committee wrote a manual that included procedures for every conceivable eventuality. These days I wonder if we might have handled the situation better by doing a lot of talking at small staff meetings, in order to inject a little more reality into the common consciousness. I mean, after all—punching "through the nose to the back of the head"? Wonder women? Bruce Lee at the Circ Desk? Mercifully, this is a section that never had to be applied. On the other hand, the resulting manual was regarded as a boon by everyone.

Our current problem situation manual (it appears as Appendix C) is a good deal more relaxed in its approach. It reflects revised assumptions about what our task is, our rights as a library staff to protect ourselves, and our knowledge that our worst and most frequent problems are going to be with angry people, not with sexual deviants or street people. We certainly contend with problems created by the latter categories, but I think the staff now has an easy confidence (based on experience and training) in its ability to handle them.

I don't know whether the transition from precise procedures to a narrative approach is evolutionary, but I do believe that the sixth edition of our manual (now called *Handling Problem Situations in the Library—A Training and Reference Manual for Staff*) is a good deal more interesting to read than the 1984 document. I have included it as an Appendix because it illustrates most of my prejudices and convictions about manual writing.

Purpose of Problem Situation Manuals

A good problem situation manual has one basic purpose: to tell staff what to do, and how to do it, when a problem comes up. It should reflect the policies and procedures upon which the staff is supposed to base its actions. That is, it should answer basic questions, such as who calls the police when an incident occurs: the staff person on the line, or a supervisor.

And it should also convey, in its basic style, how we want the staff to interact with the public. If we expect the staff to be formal, cold, and rigid in their approach, then by all means write a manual that is colorless, tight-lipped, dry, and sniffy. If we are striving for interactions with the public that are relaxed and friendly, then try to use manual language that is warmer.

A useful manual should not be a document that we thrust into the hands of a new staff person, saying, "Oh, yes, and read this by Monday—it's got a lot of good stuff you need to know." The manual has to be the basis for training of two sorts: what is provided to newcomers, and on-going discussions at staff meetings. Chapter 10 discusses training more thoroughly.

Good manuals also are organic documents. They grow and change. Sometimes they get thrown out altogether and something better substituted (see the Santa Cruz experience). One of the most important things that can come out of training discussions at regular staff meetings is information about what needs to be added or changed in the existing manual. Reviewing incident reports has the same purpose. Someone on the library's management staff should take responsibility for ensuring that the problem situation manual is kept up to date—that it addresses new problems as they arise, takes cognizance of new laws as they are passed, and is periodically freshened up with new examples or at least a new cover.

Finally, a problem situation manual has to take account of the different situations of different branches. The resources upon which a downtown branch can rely (three minute response time from the police, for example) are vastly different than those of more isolated facilities. While the basic policies must be the same, a good manual will include variable procedures which take cognizance of small branches as well as medium-size and large.

Notes on Style

Whether of the Concise genre or the Narrative, manuals should be written in the second person singular or plural, and in the active, rather than passive voice. If you mean that you want a staff person to behave or to do something in a certain way, say so directly. It is better to write,

> *Tell the patron, "No, you may not do...."*
> than
> *Patrons should be told that they may not...*

Use definite language. Avoid waffling words such as "seems," or "perhaps," or "possibly," unless of course these words are appropriate to the context. Put the topic at the beginning of the sentence, and try to keep sentences short. Do not confuse the words "may" and "can." The former means "allow" and the latter "able," as "Videos may be checked out for two days only," versus "You can check out videos at the library."

Give staff precise language to use in as many situations as you possibly can. It is not that the staff will necessarily use the language you provide—they are not automatons, after all, and we are not interested in creating a corps of robots. But having language filed away in one's head for what to say to a person who has just set off the security system alarm, ("Excuse me, but I think we forgot to check out your library materials") can be very helpful to a staff person who has just been surprised by a ringing bell while coping with a line of people waiting for service.

Writing sample language can be a useful technique for training, too. Asking a staff group to discuss a particular problem, and to come up with the best language to use in handling it, is a good way to help everyone clarify the nature of the problem, remind themselves of the library's procedure for handling it, and find words which people are comfortable using.

Content

It is very easy, when creating a problem situation manual, to get bored about two-thirds of the way through the process (or sooner), and start eliminating ideas for the contents. "Oh *surely* we don't need that level of detail," someone will argue, and out will go the information on what to do when a patron tries to get past the circulation desk with a book from which he or she has torn the barcode label.

Actually, however, the more the examples and discussions of problems there are, the better. One reason is that it is reassuring to staff who might otherwise believe that they are the only ones in the whole world who ever received an obscene phone call, or got taken to the cleaners (verbally) by an irate patron. Another reason is that people almost always respond better when they are not surprised by events. Being prepared for the unexpected in patron behavior makes for a calm response. Finally, an encyclopedic manual (or at least one which tries to cover most of the categories of problem situations staff encounter) is a good way to remind trainers of what they must cover during the orientation of new employees.

The Manual Writing Process

A very common method for getting a problem situation manual (or any other kind) written is for a staff committee to take on the job. There are good reasons for this. Probably the best one is that it involves the people on the front line, who after all have the most experience in handling problem situations, in writing up the response procedures. Provided the staff understands the library's basic philosophy and policies, the procedures they produce are likely to be far more useful than something management thinks up in a back room.

Asking a staff committee to write the manual also creates a corps of people who can serve as trainers when the manual is introduced to the rest of the staff. Moreover, they will be advocates for those procedures and methods which other staff find difficult to believe will actually work.

The trouble with a staff manual writing committee is that the process takes so long. This is especially true if the committee decides to be original, instead of adapting another library's manual to local conditions. And of course, documents developed by committee have a terrible tendency to read as though a camel actually did write them.

Here's an ideal scenario for a manual writing process. It tries to use the expertise of staff at the same time that it hurries the process along.

1. Somebody, probably the person (the Director?) who decided the staff needed a manual, should collect some examples of typical problem situation man-

uals from other libraries. The samples in Appendix C suggest some places to write, and the whole Santa Cruz manual is there too. Any library is free to copy it (with appropriate credit, of course).

2. A small committee of staff, led by a senior manager, but including a floor supervisor or someone from the public service desks, should be appointed. If your library is a multi-branch system, find a way to include a staff person from one of the smaller branches, who can speak to the issue of what works when you are on your own. The Committee's first task is to review the manuals, decide on a format (concise or narrative), and agree on whether the sample manuals from other libraries can be adapted to local needs. Based on this decision, the committee should develop a time schedule for completing a draft manual.

3. Assuming an adaptation of an existing manual, the committee should decide on the contents. What problem situations does this library need to be sure to cover?

4. Then, it should review each section of the model to be used, and identify the problem situation areas for which the library lacks policy. These should be taken to the Director and management staff for guidance, plus a reminder of what the production schedule for the manual is.

5. While management staff works on needed policies, the Manual Committee can work on revising the sample manual's procedures to fit the local situation. The senior manager should assign sections to each person, so that the committee doesn't start talking as a group about a procedure until it has a first draft with which to work.

   Here's where consultation with line staff is absolutely crucial. If a committee member is assigned the section on handling a rowdy drunk, for instance, or someone spaced out on drugs, that person should interview the desk worker who last dealt with such a problem. What did s/he say? How did s/he get the person out the door? Did her/his actions match library policy? Try the sample manual's procedures on the desk worker, and see whether s/he thinks they are a fair rendition of what should be done.

   The next step is to write a draft, and take it back to the people on the line. Revisions should be based on their comments. It is certainly possible that staff informants are not going to have creative ideas for words to use in a difficult situation, or other suggestions. If this is the case, the committee will need to think up the proper language for what to say or do.

6. The committee will probably also want to consult with the local police department for advice on techniques and procedures.

7. The director and others also should be consulting with staff as they work on developing the missing policies upon which procedures are based. Fre-

quently, by the time a policy has been negotiated, the procedures for implementing it are obvious. But be careful here. It is a trap to think that writing up a good statement of the library's policy is the same as thinking through and writing out careful procedures for implementing it. The manual, after all, is aimed at all workers, from the youngest and least sophisticated page to senior reference staff.

8. The completed first draft probably needs to be reviewed by the director or whatever other senior managers exist. A meeting to discuss revisions is frequently helpful. It gives the director an opportunity to say directly why s/he doesn't like a procedure being proposed, and the committee a chance to argue back in favor of methods the staff feels strongly about.

9. The next stop might be the office of the jurisdiction's legal counsel. The director should initiate this, and be prepared to argue for flexibility and for the library's mission.

10. After a clean-up revision based on these reviews, send the manual out to various of the library's key departments or supervisors. Be sure to include branches of various sizes. Set deadlines for response, and if it looks like there is going to be a lot of trouble (as, "Well, I'm sorry, but that is **not** the way we do it at the Mostly Branch"), get everyone together for a "Let's trash the draft manual" session. Think of it as the first round in the training process.

11. All these drafts will have revealed some of the formatting options provided by your word processing equipment or creative staff typists. The object is to make the manual easy to read and use (or accessible, as we say in the library business), as well as attractive. Strive for openness, clarity of organization, and lots of white space.

   Three ring binders are a frequent cover choice, because they make updating simple. On the other hand, if you guess that you are going to need a new edition every year anyway, and really want to be able to give every single staff person his or her own copy, it might be less expensive to stick with comb binding or staples.

12. With a final document in hand, discuss how to introduce it to all staff, training them on its contents and use. See the next chapter for some suggestions on how to do this, and particularly for the role of the hardworking Manual Committee, which in my ideal scenario, does not get to disband for another twelve months at least. And boy, do they love that. Committees groan like camels, too.

Chapter 10

Training Staff

I previewed a wonderful training video recently. It is called "Give 'Em the Pickle!" with Bob Farrell, who owns restaurants and trains mostly corporate audiences in customer service techiques.[1]

Farrell talks about asking workers to pretend they are actors and play the part of a really good waitress or an excellent circulation desk worker. This enables the worker to play the role even when she or he feels lousy, and has the effect of persuading the public to play a role themselves—that of satisfied customers, because they are.

Farrell's technique reminded me of two very important points made by the literature of education. The first is the distinction between education and training.[2] Education is what we learn for the long term. It is useful whether one's job changes or not. Among other things, it enables us to analyze and extrapolate even as conditions change. Training, on the other hand, teaches skills for a particular time and place. The payoff is immediate.

The other important point is that adults learn best when the learning is based on their experience.[3] You can lecture at them all you like, but if you really want them to get the message, you have to put the material in the context of what they already know. Or, as the title of a very useful book by Harold Stolovitch and Erica Keeps puts it, *Telling Ain't Training*.[4] If they don't have relevant experience, then it is wise to find a technique, such as role playing, which gives them experience on the spot. This is the reason I was interested in Bob Farrell's acting technique.

When librarians talk about training staff at least one of our objectives is inculcating workers with the library's organizational culture or style. That applies whether the focus of the training is problem situations or just everyday interaction with the public. We work hard to hire people who seem as though they have what it takes to make it on the front desk. But then our obligation is to give them the information and skills they need to do the work, and do it in a way that matches our conception of the kind of place our public library is supposed to be.

That conception will not be the same for all public libraries, nor indeed for all the branches within a single library system. Service at a tiny neighborhood branch, where the staff is likely to know the names of most of the regulars, *and* their grandchildren, is different from the style at the downtown library, where there is almost always a line of two or three people waiting to use the Internet access terminals. Basic style for interacting with the public is modified by the circumstances of daily reality. Nevertheless, conveying what the library is after in its relations with patrons, whatever that may be, is a basic objective of training.

Underneath the somewhat loosely and variably defined umbrella of "style," however, there are three basic objectives that any effective problem situation training program will feature: ensuring that staff knows and understands library policies and procedures, teaching appropriate skills for implementing those policies and procedures, and providing a means for on-going discussion and communication about problem situations.

Training New Workers

My definition of heaven is a place where every writer of letters to the editor of the local newspaper who proposes that the public library can be run with volunteers has to take the initial training we give to each library clerk who joins our regular staff. If the letter writer doesn't fall apart over automation system procedures for handling requests, s/he will certainly flunk when s/he gets to skills for telling a patron that they can't check out any more videos until they pay off the $9.99 they owe in back fines.

Most libraries, even the smallest and poorest, invest an incredible number hours in teaching new staff the technical basics of their work, whether it is circulation desk procedures or reference clerical support. Many of them attempt to dedicate training time to personal communication skills, as well, and to procedures for handling problems created by difficult patron behavior.

I think it is fair to say, however, that as our automation systems grow more complex, and the number of services staff can provide to the public increases, more time *must* be spent on technical training. Skill in handling problem situations is increasingly left to on-the-job mentoring by supervisors.

One way to compensate is to have a good problem situation manual, which can be used to back up a minimal training session (say an hour?) on "how we handle problem situations at this library." Giving a lengthy manual to a new staff person to read is one way of saying, "This is what happens here; this is how we try to do things."

It can also be a means, alas, for scaring the daylights out of the newcomer. The less sophisticated ones will not let too much time pass before they whisper to a new colleague, "Are they kidding? Does stuff like this *really* go on here?" Yes, is the answer, it does, and the sooner new workers understand that, the sooner they will be competent on the public desks. I once heard a library director remark that one of the *purposes* of new staff training is to let them know that public libraries are *not* necessarily pleasant places in which to work.

At any rate, the frequent outcome of the pressure to teach as much as we can in a short time is that we send new people to the public desks with only sketchy training in problem situation handling, but a reasonably thorough understanding of the worst they can expect from the library users. It is therefore very important to make sure that the workers' supervisors take responsibility for completing the training process. The first part of this needs to be a reality check ("No, dear, the majority of our patrons are very nice people, *really*."). And there probably should be a checklist of discussions and experiences for the worker.

One on-the-job training device is to partner the new worker with someone more experienced. Indeed, it is a good idea to appoint an official mentor for every new person who joins the staff. The mentor's job is give the newcomer the inside scoop on all the things missed in training (why the soft drink machine only takes quarters) and to be responsible for showing her or him the real score, as opposed to the theoretical one taught in training.

The other important mentoring task is to make sure the novice gets a chance to observe a more senior staff member handling (for example) an angry patron, and *talk about it afterwards*. Was "stand and deliver" necessary in this case, or did paraphrasing work? Is the worker satisfied with the outcome of the encounter, or does s/he feel in retrospect that she could have done better? This kind of debriefing exercise makes all workers conscious of how they are handling stressful encounters, and establishes the pattern of communication among co-workers that is crucial to effective management of difficult situations.

Most organizations have performance appraisal processes built into their personnel regulations, sometimes including three month and six month probationary evaluations. Unfortunately, the appraisals are all too frequently based on standardized municipal forms, meant to be used for all classes of employees, from trash collectors to library clerks. This makes it difficult for a line supervisor to use appraisal as tool for improving individual employee performance. At the very least, however, the appraisal interview can be a time for talking with a new worker about problem situation experiences, and providing some advice and instruction. The performance objectives that ought to be part of the appraisal can include things such as re-reading and thinking about a section of the manual; observation; or practicing a particular skill with another worker.

Finally, of course, it is important to give new workers off-desk time to do the manual reading and one-on-one practice with other staff that is necessary for training. No one would deny how difficult this can be in a busy library, but it is important.

On-Going Staff Training

At a recent state library conference I entertained myself by asking my colleagues how much time they put into on-going staff training in handling problem situations. Although several cited day-long staff workshops (organized by their own libraries or by a regional consortium), the majority response was eyes raised to heaven.

"I know, I know." said one. "We should be keeping people's skills sharp on this. And problems are getting more frequent, too. We have a manual, and I know people are using it. But honestly! There just doesn't seem to be time for more than that."

I followed up by asking whether building a short period of problem situation training into every staff meeting would be a useful device. Most thought it might be, but they were not entirely sure how the line supervisors would take to it. Staff meeting time is short too, with heavy agendas built into tiny windows of time between getting the book drop cleared and opening for the day.

In Chapter 2 I suggested the "Ten Minutes a Week for Training" model because I am convinced that frequent talk about problem situations is a crucial method of helping staff deal with them effectively.

Sharing the experience of long-term staff and relieving stress by the therapy of talking are only two of the more obvious reasons. I also suggested that a good staff discussion of a bad situation provided management with invaluable insight into what is actually happening on the library floor.

An underlying theme of this book has been that effective handling of problem situations depends upon open communication among workers. People in one department or branch must have opportunities to tell each other when curious or difficult incidents take place, if only to provide alerts as to what may be coming down next. This is not simply passing around Polaroid pictures of known flashers, so everyone can be alert to the potential problem. It is also sharing information so that collective solutions can be found.

The branch manager who has never had to deal with a highly verbal, mentally ill street person can be coached through the trauma by staff who have, *if they know it is happening to her.* But unless mechanisms for public (e.g. staff meeting or e-mail) discussion of problem situations are built into ongoing library life, this might not happen. Of course the afflicted branch manager will talk about it to her staff friends, but "whine" about it at an open staff meeting? Forget it, unless talk is part of the normal operating mode.

The major problem with the Ten Minutes a Week for Training idea is limiting it to ten minutes. I am pretty sure, however, that if a supervisor finds her/himself with a problem situation discussion which staff are unwilling to terminate, then the technique has done what it is supposed to: opened a window on a problem that people need to talk about. I also think that as problem situation discussions become routine, it will be easier for staff to limit their talking time.

Each of the preceding problem situation chapters provided discussion questions or incidents for staff meeting use. A staff getting into the spirit of the thing will have little trouble thinking up variations that reflect local conditions. And the suggestions are not meant to substitute for a report and discussion of an actual incident and how the staff involved handled it.

Many libraries are lucky enough to have a senior manager who is responsible for staff training—coordinating who gets to go where to learn what, and how new hires are taken through the standard training process. In smaller operations, this is one of the many balls that the library director must juggle. In either case, it is a good idea to have an on-going *annual training plan*. The plan helps keep track of when the staff last discussed handling sexual deviancy cases, for instance, or how many months it has been since everyone was "refreshed" on the procedures for responding to book complaints. Given that there are other training issues to be worked into the standard calendar (periodic reviews of emergency procedures, for example), it becomes very important to systematize this process.

Workshops as a Training Technique

Organizing a half-day or an all-day workshop for training is a popular way to get the job done, and has many advantages. For one thing, attending the workshop gets people out of the library, or at least off the public desks. And when the workshop brings staff from several libraries together, it can be especially interesting.

On the other hand, a workshop organized by a regional consortium limits the number of people who can attend, so it can't be relied upon as the primary training tool. The best that one can hope for is that staff who attend will bring the information home and share it with those left behind.

Several good books have been written about organizing workshops. I think one of the most interesting is Robert L. Jolles' *How to Run Seminars and Workshops*, which is aimed at trainers. But he also offers a lot of practical advice on organization and presentation.[5] One of the basic points all authors make is that it is crucial to be very clear about both the purpose and the audience for the workshop.

A half-day regional workshop called something like, "Handling Problem Situations in the Library," is, to my mind, doomed to failure. The topic is far too broad. Most participants will go away with an expanded knowledge of the infinite and varied problems library staffs face, but not many new skills in how to handle them.

On the other hand, a workshop that aims to improve the skills of people in handling angry or irate patrons offers a chance for real learning. It can be organized to focus on teaching two or three skills (active listening, for example), with plenty of time for group practice built in.

So limiting the topic is very important. So is understanding who the audience will be, and whether what they need is education or skills. If a group of support staff from different libraries have never gotten together before, nor had the chance to talk to each other about how tough life is on the front desk, a workshop structured to provide background information on the homeless problem in America—except in brief, clear, capsule form—is a waste of effort. What this group needs is a chance to share experiences, to talk about what works in certain situations and what doesn't, and the opportunity to acquire some specific new skills.

On the other hand, offering a workshop aimed at broadening the knowledge of youth services workers about the needs of immigrant children is a different kettle of fish entirely. Here a speaker providing overview information and analysis, coupled with presentations on different ideas for service, might be useful for everyone.

HINTS FOR ORGANIZING BETTER WORKSHOPS

First, make sure that everyone understands, up front, what the purpose of the workshop is, how it will be conducted, what will happen when, and where the restrooms are. Guarantee the time when breaks and lunch will occur, and stick to the announced schedule, even if this means interrupting a hot discussion (or if it's *really* hot, at least poll the participants before postponing a break). A third of the crowd will be grateful, I promise.

Plan the internal schedule of the workshop carefully, allowing plenty of flex time for discussions to run over *without* affecting breaks. Assume that it will not actually get started on time, but don't let the delay be more than ten minutes, or you risk annoying all the people who were prompt. Also assume that you will lose the audience, in spirit if not in fact, at 4 P.M., especially if the participants have come from someplace else, and are therefore worried about the evening commute home.

If the workshop is meant to teach skills, make sure the time allocations match the following general pattern: 15 percent for explaining the skill, 25 percent for demonstrating it, and 60 percent for engaging the trainees in guided practice.[6] Robert Jolles offers the following "old saying" as an additional guide:

What people hear, they forget.
What people see, they remember.
What people do, they learn.[7]

An education workshop, on the other hand, will spend far more time on lecturing, demonstration, discussion, and debate, with only perhaps 25 percent of the time allocated to small group work and consolidation of what has been learned.

If you are going to have a speaker, be careful whom you invite. Make sure someone whose judgment you trust has actually heard the speaker, and vouches for his/her effectiveness. Be sure that you and the speaker/instructor agree on both the methodology for teaching a skill, and how much time will be required. For example, I would look askance at anyone who offers to teach active listening skills in one hour, and proposes to do it via an overhead projector and handouts.

If the topic is broader, you will want to be sure that the speaker knows what is expected of her or him. Write it down in your confirmation letter, and be sure to include a description of who the participants are going to be. Nothing can ruin a workshop faster than a speaker who misjudges the audience, tells bad when-I-was-a-youngster-in-the-library jokes, and rambles away from the point of the session.

Finally, move heaven and earth to find a workshop location that is big and comfortable enough—for both the whole group sessions and smaller groups. It is in accommodating the latter that so many workshop spaces are inadequate: four small groups meeting in the four corners of a room can be deafening for everyone. Look at how much time is going to be spent in small groups, and make acquiring space for that aspect a priority.

Introducing the New Manual

Closing down the library and holding an all day workshop for staff can be a lot of fun for everyone, and is the ideal way to introduce a new manual on handling problem situations. The staff committee that wrote the manual (see Chapter 9) can be assigned the task of organizing this event. Here's one scenario for such a workshop.

Distribute the manual to every member of the staff two or three days, or even a week, before the workshop, with a request that they read it, and think about it. Many will not, of course, because they won't have time, but at least the document is in people's hands and has become somewhat familiar.

Open the workshop with a "nuts and bolts of the day" talk by the staff chair of the Manual Committee: the time of breaks, the arrangements for lunch, and so forth. Then introduce the director for a brief (ten minutes?) pep talk on the library's philosophy of service, what its behavior rules are, and the style the new manual uses in patron relations. It is very important that the imprimatur of official management support be given to the manual.

It is also important, and okay, to interrupt the director with the first of a series of demonstrations of difficult behavior, acted out by staff. For example, get a senior manager wearing a backwards baseball cap and a dirty tee shirt to skateboard down the center aisle of the meeting room, playing a boom box at top volume. How the director copes with the interruption (either badly or well) doesn't much matter, so long as everyone laughs, and listens to the explanation of how such an incident ought to be handled.

The rest of the day should be organized into the following pattern. Decide on the four or five most important sections of the manual, based on which problem situations are most difficult or frightening to staff. Then allocate a block of time for each of them. Introduce each difficult behavior with a role-played example, followed by a brief discussion with the audience of what was right or wrong about how the incident was handled. Talk about the right way, and then break everyone into small groups (no more than six people) for fifteen minutes of practice. Set the small groups up with three practice situations each (they can be the same for all groups), ask people to act out the roles, and discuss how each team handled the problem. If yours is a multi-branch system, find a way to group people who work in branches of the same size.

After the practice session, get everyone back together for questions, and for more explanation of the theory or background on the problem. This is the moment, for example, for a member of the Manual Committee to do five minutes on the problems caused by de-institutionalization of the mentally ill, and the local community's response.

Conclude the day with a final debriefing and question-and-answer session. If serious problems about understanding a policy have emerged during the day, try to deal with them here. It is best, of course, to end on a high note— perhaps a final pep talk by the director. In Santa Cruz, we traditionally end with wine and cheese. (But then, this is coastal California.)

Role-playing is a very important methodology for this kind of workshop. As a training tool, it gives people experience and practice in coping with problem situations, and in saying things that do not necessarily come easily to them. Moreover, in small group practice sessions, it is hard for even the shyest or most stubbornly silent person to avoid participating.

As for the role-playing that introduces each problem situation module, the more exalted the staff members acting out roles, the more fun all the workshop participants will have. Few things in library life are more enjoyable than watching the director of libraries make a fool of herself pretending to be a street person who smells bad. And it can be a useful experience for the head of youth services to act out the role of an indignant parent who wants to know why on earth the library has a copy of *Heather Has Two Mommies*.

Every library staff (indeed, every group of people) has its nay sayers and negative talkers who do their best (or so the leader feels) to sabotage the carefully constructed pattern of the meeting or training session. They range from the ones who dominate the group by talking too much to those who refuse to believe that a new procedure is going to work, and stubbornly keep on saying so.

Jolles in *How to Run Seminars and Workshops* offers smart advice for how to handle these kinds of problems, which needn't be reiterated here. But this does bring up the continuing role of the Manual Committee. One thing the committee chair can say is, "You could be right. This may not work, although we think it will. But during the next year we are all going to be testing these procedures, and talking about how they work. What's the worst that can happen? If they don't work, we'll think up something better."

There are two points here. The first is that theoretically no procedures should be put into place without first testing them. And that is an easy rule to follow when the subject is a concrete one, such as how to register a borrower on the new automation system. But people, and how they act, are not concrete. They are infinitely varied in their behavior, requiring flexibility of response by staff when the behavior causes a problem.

This means that while we can work out the best procedure we can think of, and run it by as many staff people as possible for comment before we "publish" it, we are never going to be certain that it is the best one until it has been used for a period of time. Therefore, we have to set up a mechanism for reporting on how the procedures in the new manual work, and evaluating those reports. And if procedures *don't* work, the Committee has to be prepared to throw out even their very favorites, and start again.

The second point is the conclusion of this chapter and book. Problem situations in libraries seem to run a pattern. In fact, they are so usual that they are boring. There will always be angry people, the occasional drunk, and kids who get too rambunctious. And there will be flashers, stalkers, molesters, porn viewers, stinkers, and people who want to challenge the contents of the collections. These we can anticipate, and train the staff to handle. It is the surprises that are the hard part, although they do keep library life interesting.

Fundamentally, these difficult times leave us with two options. We can allow ourselves to be frightened by a changing world, and reassure ourselves by setting up a structure of rules and procedures that turn our libraries into armed fortresses. Or, we can accept the fact that the unexpected and different comes with the territory, do the very best to prepare for both, and rely on our common sense, and that of our staffs, to handle whatever happens.

That's the course I urge. It's hard work. And the staff members and administrators who occupy the bedeviled territory of library work are in many ways the unsung heroines and heroes of the common culture. The territory in question is the people's place, even when they don't treat it right. It is the vital informational base for our evolving democracy. It is a territory that it is crucially necessary to hold open and free.

Perhaps the greatest irony in the situation is that as society's problems bear in ever more strenuously on public libraries, the steps we take to make it possible for maximum use of the collections and resources by *everybody* will increasingly also bring complaints about our attempts to be even-handed.

Thus, the contradiction: especially when we do the job well, there are fewer and fewer to thank us. We just have to remember that our work, in the aggregate, is of incalculable importance. Every day, libraries keep the nation's information in motion, keep the society literate and informed. Take libraries away from the people—all the people—and from the social process, and our nation would be in a very bad way indeed.

This book expresses my deep admiration and respect for library workers—sentiments that I know are shared throughout our profession. When times are tough, it's good to stop and remember that that comes with the territory too.

Notes

Chapter 1

1. I am very grateful to the following attorneys for providing advice and comments on this chapter: John Barisone, City Attorney of the City of Santa Cruz, Chris Hansen, Staff Counsel, American Civil Liberties Union, New York, and Mary Minow, Library Law, Inc., Cupertino, California.

2. Mary Minow, e-mail message 08/20/03.

3. *Richard R. Kreimer v. Bureau of Police for the Town of Morristown et al, Free Public Library of Morristown and Morris Township et al*, 959 F. 2d 1242, No. 91-5501, U.S. Court of Appeals for the Third Circuit, decided March 23, 1991. Hereinafter cited as *Kreimer v. Morristown.*

4. *Kreimer v. Morristown.* [p. 23].

5. *Ibid.*

6. *Armstrong v. District of Columbia Public Library*, 154 F. Supp 2d 67 (2001). Cited and explicated in Mary Minow, "Patron Behavior Rules in Libraries: Reported Court Cases."

7. *Ibid.*

8. Bruce Ennis, Esq., "Patron Behavior and Access to Information: The Legal Issues." Speech presented at Public Library Association Hot Topics Program, American Library Association Annual Conference, San Francisco, California, June 30, 1992.

9. You might want to provide your attorney with a copy of an excellent ALA resource, *The Library's Legal Answer Book* by Mary Minow and Tomas A. Lipinsky (Chicago: American Library Association, 2003).

Chapter 2

1. Blau, Joel. *The Visible Poor—Homelessness in the United States.* New York: Oxford University Press, 1992.

2. Woodrum, Pat. "A Haven for the Homeless." *Library Journal,* V. 113, January 1988, p. 55–57.

3. Parker, Richard. E-mail to the author. July 24, 2003.

Chapter 3

1. Crowe, Sandra A. *Since Strangling Isn't an Option ... Dealing with Difficult People—Common Problems and Uncommon Solutions.* New York: Penguin Putnam, Inc., 1999.

2. Smith, Nathan M. and Irene Adams. "Using Active Listening to Deal with Patron Problems." *Public Libraries,* July/August 1991, p. 236.

Chapter 4

1. The definitions of deviant behavior used in this chapter are taken from American Psychiatric Association, *Diagnostic and Statistical Manual of Mental Disorders*, Fourth Edition, Text Revision. Washington, D.C.: American Psychiatric Association, 2000.

2. *Ibid.*, p. 571.

3. Laning, Kenneth V. "Child Molesters: A Behavioral Analysis for Law Enforcement

Officers Investigating Cases of Child Sexual Exploitation." April 1987, in U.S. Department of Justice, Federal Bureau of Investigation. *Deviant and Criminal Sexuality.* Quantico, Virginia: National Center for the Analysis of Violent Crime, 1991.

4. The author is extremely grateful to Meredith Pierce and the staff of the Alachua County Library for permission to quote Ms. Pierce extensively on an incident which caused her much pain and anxiety.

5. City of Santa Cruz Administrative Procedure Order Section II, #1A (Revised October 1, 1999).

6. Santa Cruz City County Library System. *Handling Problem Situations in the Library.* 6th Edition, December 2002.

Quotations in this chapter are based on the following telephone interviews with the author: Linda Luke, Alachua County Library, Gainesville, Florida, September 1, 1992; Carole Hildebrand, Director, Eugene (Oregon) Public Library, September 1, 1992; Meredith Pierce, Alachua County Library, Gainesville, Florida, September 1, 1991. The author is also grateful to Ricardo Alcaino, Analyst in the City of Santa Cruz Human Resources Department, and Santa Cruz Library Assistant Director Susan Elgin, for consultation on the section about creating an harassment-free workplace for library workers.

Chapter 5

1. *Unattended Children in the Public Library: A Resource Guide.* Published by the Association for Library Service to Children, the Association for Library Trustees and Advocates, The Public Library Association. Chicago, Illinois, 2000.

2. White, Herbert S. "Pseudo-libraries and semi-teachers." Part 1. *American Libraries*, Vol. 21, No. 2 February 1990, p. 106.

3. *"Latchkey Children" in the Public Library: A Position Paper.* Prepared by the Service to Children Committee of the Public Library Association in Collaboration with the Library Service to Children with Special Needs Committee of the Association for Library Service to Children. Chicago: May 1988, p. 12.

4. *Ibid.*, p. 12.

5. Sandra Nelson for the Public Library Association. *The New Planning for Results,*

A Streamlined Approach. Chicago: American Library Association, 2001.

6. *Unattended Children in the Public Library: A Resource Guide*, p. 32–39.

7. Santa Clara (CA) County Library. "Santa Clara County Library Procedures Manual," April 1, 1984. Part A, Section 501.1, B.1 & B.1.

8. Dowd, Frances Smardo. *Latchkey Children in the Library & Community.* Phoenix, Arizona: Oryx Press, 1991.

9. *Unattended Children in the Public Library: A Resource Guide*, p. 23–24.

Chapter 6

1. "Harry Potter series tops list of most challenged books four years in a row." Release of January 13, 2003. *Challenged and Banned Books.* Office of Intellectual Freedom. 18 September 2003 http://www.ala.org/Our_Association/Offices/Intellectual_Freedom.

2. *Ibid.*

3. *Intellectual Freedom Manual* compiled by the Office of Intellectual Freedom of the American Library Association. 6th ed. Chicago: American Library Association, 2002.

4. *Ibid.*, p. 340–41.

5. American Library Association. *Library Bill of Rights.* Adopted June 18, 1948, amended February 2, 1961, June 27, 1967, and January 23, 1980 by the ALA Council.

6. Associated Press Service, 09/10/92: PM-*Daddy's Roommate*, 0610. "Children's Book About Gay Parent Creating Uproar." By Sue Price Wilson, Associated Press Writer.

7. Blume, Judy. "Censors; Judy talks about her experiences." JudyBlume.com. 18 September 2003 http://www.JudyBlume.com.

Chapter 7

1. Adamson, Wendy. "Sex in the City: What Happened at the Minneapolis Public Library." *Off Our Backs,* Sept-Oct 2002, p. 2.

2. Mark Smith, ed. *Managing the Internet Controversy.* New York: Neal-Schuman Publishers, Inc., 2001.

3. *Intellectual Freedom Manual* compiled by the Office of Intellectual Freedom of the

American Library Association. 6th ed. Chicago: American Library Association, 2002.

4. *Managing the Internet Controversy*, p. 83–101.

5. Hildreth, Susan. E-mail to the author. 22 July 2003.

6. *Intellectual Freedom Manual*, p. 287–288.

7. *United States v. American Library Association, Inc.* No. 02-361, 123 S.Ct. 2297, 2003 WL 21433656 (June 23, 2003).

8. See for example, "Internet Blocking in Public Schools," a study by the Electronic Frontier Foundation and the Online Policy Group. Version 1.1, 26 June 2003, or "Kaiser Study: Filters Impede Health Research," *American Libraries*, January 2003, 20.

9. *Intellectual Freedom Manual*, p. 291. An article by Cynthia K. Richey, "Molding Effective Internet Policies," *Computers in Libraries*, Vol. 22, Issue 6, June 2002, p. 16 is an interesting account of how one library devised its policy, and it offers an excellent list of sources for additional reading.

Chapter 8

1. *Library Security Guidelines Document*, June 7, 2001. American Library Association, LAMA Buildings and Equipment Section, Security Guidelines Subcommittee of the Safety and Security in Library Buildings Committee. This very useful set of guidelines covers virtually all security issues from fire and emergency protection to alarms and electronics. Suggested security staff qualifications and staff pre-employment screening guidelines are included in Appendices.

Chapter 10

1. Farrell, Bob. "Give 'em the Pickle!" GIV 19VHS Advanced Training Source, n.d.

2. Davies, Ivor K. *Instructional Technique*. New York: McGraw Hill Book Company, 1981. p. 20.

3. Knowles, Malcolm, Elwood F. Holton III, Richard A. Swanson. *The Adult Learner: The Definitive Classic in Adult Education and Human Resource Development*. Houston, Texas: Gulf Publishing Co., 1998 p. 35–72.

4. Stolovitch, Harold D. and Erica J. Keeps. *Telling Ain't Training*. Alexandria, Virginia: American Society for Training and Development, 2001.

5. Jolles, Robert L. *How to Run Seminars and Workshops*. 2nd edition. New York: John Wiley and Sons, Inc. 2001. Another useful source on organizing workshops is Klatt, Bruce. *The Ultimate Training Workshop Handbook*. New York: McGraw Hill, 1999.

6. Davies, p. 50.

7. Jolles, p. 11.

Appendices

Appendix A

The Library Bill of Rights

The American Library Association affirms that all libraries are forums for information and ideas, and that the following basic policies should guide their services.

I. Books and other library resources should be provided for the interest, information, and enlightenment of all people of the community the library serves. Materials should not be excluded because of the origin, background, or views of those contributing to their creation.

II. Libraries should provide materials and information presenting all points of view on current and historical issues. Materials should not be proscribed or removed because of partisan or doctrinal disapproval.

III. Libraries should challenge censorship in the fulfillment of their responsibility to provide information and enlightenment.

IV. Libraries should cooperate with all persons and groups concerned with resisting abridgment of free expression and free access to ideas.

V. A person's right to use a library should not be denied or abridged because of origin, age, background, or views.

VI. Libraries which make exhibit spaces and meeting rooms available to the public they serve should make such facilities available on an equitable basis, regardless of the beliefs or affiliations of individuals or groups requesting their use.

Adopted June 18, 1948. Amended by the ALA Council February 2, 1961; June 27, 1967; and January 23, 1980, inclusion of "age" reaffirmed January 23, 1996.

Appendix B

Guidelines for the Development of Policies and Procedures Regarding User Behavior and Library Usage

Libraries are faced with problems of user behavior that must be addressed to insure the effective delivery of service and full access to facilities. Library governing bodies must approach the regulation of user behavior within the framework of the ALA "Code of Ethics," the *Library Bill of Rights*, and the law, including local and state statues, constitutional standards under the First and Fourteenth Amendments, due process and equal treatment under the law.

Publicly supported library service is based upon the First Amendment right of free expression. Publicly supported libraries are recognized as limited public forums for access to information. At least one federal court of appeals has recognized a First Amendment right to receive information in a public library. Library policies and procedures that could impinge upon such rights are subject to a higher standard of review than may be required in the policies of other public services and facilities.

There is a significant government interest in maintaining a library environment that is conducive to all users' exercise of their constitutionally protected right to receive information. This significant interest authorizes publicly supported libraries to maintain a safe and healthy environment in which library users and staff can be free from harassment, intimidation, and threats to their safety and well-being. Libraries should provide appropriate safeguards against such behavior and enforce policies and procedures addressing that behavior when it occurs.

In order to protect all library users' right of access to library facilities, to ensure the safety of users and staff, and to protect library resources and facilities from damage, the library's governing authority may impose reasonable restrictions on the time, place, or manner of library access.

GUIDELINES

The American Library Association's Intellectual Freedom Committee recommends that publicly supported libraries use the following guidelines, based upon constitutional principles, to develop policies and procedures governing the use of library facilities:

1. Libraries are advised to rely upon existing legislation and law enforcement mechanisms as the primary means of controlling behavior that involves public safety, criminal behavior, or other issues covered by existing local, state, or federal statutes. In many instances, this legal framework may be sufficient to provide the library with the necessary tools to maintain order.

2. If the library's governing body chooses to write its own policies and procedures regarding user behavior or access to library facilities, services, and resources, the policies should cite statutes or ordinances upon which the authority to make those policies is based.

3. Library policies and procedures governing the use of library facilities should be carefully examined to insure that they are not in violation of the *Library Bill of Rights.*

4. Reasonably and narrowly drawn policies and procedures designed to prohibit interference with use of the facilities and services by others, or to prohibit activities inconsistent with the achievement of the library's mission statement and objectives, are acceptable.

5. Such policies and the attendant implementing procedures should be reviewed frequently and updated as needed by the library's legal counsel for compliance with federal and state constitutional requirements, federal and state civil rights legislation, all other applicable federal and state legislation, and applicable case law.

6. Every effort should be made to respond to potentially difficult circumstances of user behavior in a timely, direct, and open manner. Common sense, reason, and sensitivity should be used to resolve issues in a constructive and positive manner without escalation.

7. Libraries should develop an ongoing staff training program based upon their user behavior policy. This program should include training to develop empathy and understanding of the social and economic problems of some library users.

8. Policies and regulations that impose restrictions on library access:

a. should apply only to those activities that materially interfere with the public's right of access to library facilities, the safety of users and staff, and the protection of library resources and facilities;

b. should narrowly tailor prohibitions or restrictions so that they are not more restrictive than needed to serve their objectives;

c. should attempt to balance competing interests and avoid favoring the majority at the expense of individual rights, or allowing individual users' rights to supersede those of the majority of users;

d. should be based solely upon actual behavior and not upon arbitrary distinctions between individuals or classes of individuals. Policies should not target specific users or groups of users based upon an assumption or expectation that such users might engage in behaviors that could disrupt library service;

e. should not restrict access to the library by persons who merely inspire the anger or annoyance of others. Policies based upon appearance or behavior that is merely annoying or which merely generates negative subjective reactions from others, do not meet the necessary standard. Such policies should employ a reasonable, objective standard based on the behavior itself;

f. must provide a clear description of the behavior that is prohibited and the various enforcement measures in place, so that a reasonably intelligent person will have both due process and fair warning; this description must be continuously and clearly communicated in an effective manner to all library users;

g. to the extent possible, should not leave those affected without adequate alternative means of access to information in the library;

h. must be enforced evenhandedly, and not in a manner intended to benefit or disfavor any person or group in an arbitrary or capricious manner.

The user behaviors addressed in these Guidelines are the result of a wide variety of individual and societal conditions. Libraries should take advantage of the expertise of local social service agencies, advocacy groups, mental health professionals, law enforcement officials, and other community resources to develop community strategies for addressing the needs of a diverse population.

Adopted January 24, 1993, by the ALA Intellectual Freedom Committee; revised November 17, 2000. Reprinted by permission of the American Library Association.

Appendix C

Sample Procedures and Policies

The following pages contain the complete text of the Santa Cruz City County Library System's staff manual, *Handling Problem Situations in the Library—A Training and Reference Manual for Staff*.

Some policies and procedures from other libraries are also included. For convenience, they are interleaved in the Santa Cruz Manual but in another typeface, for ease of differentation, as noted in the Table of Contents.

HANDLING PROBLEM SITUATIONS IN THE LIBRARY: A TRAINING AND REFERENCE MANUAL FOR STAFF JANUARY 2003

TABLE OF CONTENTS

Problem Situations Defined

Problem situations, or behavior that creates a problem situation, are acts by library users which interfere with someone else's right to use the library.

> Problem behavior by library users is the specific subject of this manual, but it should be remembered that library staff and library equipment can also exhibit problem behavior. We do our best to ensure that staff do that as infrequently as possible. But occasional equipment glitches must be endured.

> This manual concerns *problem situations created by people*. Natural disasters, such as earthquake, flood, fire, or physical injury are covered in the Emergency Plans for each Branch.

Library Policy

The cornerstone of the Santa Cruz City County Library System's user behavior policy is that *no one has the right to interfere with anyone else's right to use the library.* We try to make as few specific behavior rules as possible for two reasons:

- because the library is very serious about practicing tolerance for the differences among people—not just their race or ethnicity or age or sexual preference, but in their life styles and behaviors.

- because it is impossible to anticipate every behavior which might interfere with someone else's right to use the library.

It is also the Library's policy to enforce its standards of behavior as equitably as possible among people of all ages, all economic levels, and all appearances. We do not make judgments on the basis of how people look or dress, any more than we question their right to seek any information they wish.

Four Basic Rules

Respect, Courtesy, Calm, and Tact Are Our Watchwords
The Common Sense Rule Applies
Use Teamwork with Other Staff Whenever You Can
Communicate with Your Colleagues

Staff should deal with the public with *respect, courtesy, tact, and calm*. It is important to understand that there is no simple "recipe" for solutions to all problems. Some people may cause problems by simply sitting and crying, while others are hostile, abusive, or even violent. The way in which the staff approaches the situation should depend to a large extent on the type of behavior the person is exhibiting. The next section of this manual contains specific coping techniques for some, but by no means all of the situations which public library workers may experience.

Because of the uniqueness of each situation *common sense* should play a large part in any encounter. Common sense is defined by the dictionary as "sound and prudent (but often unsophisticated) judgment." Possessing common sense is a basic requirement for working in a public library. We may all be very sophisticated in our knowledge of computers or books, but it is our sound and prudent judgment that deals with a difficult drunk, or helps a child in distress. Read this manual and learn the procedures. But when in doubt, use your common sense.

Most workers' instincts will tell them when to be sympathetic or when to back off if a patron is potentially violent. But whatever the case, handling problems should involve *teamwork*: Whenever you can, call on other staff to back you up.

Teamwork also means *communicating with your colleagues*. Often, staff can collectively develop effective responses to difficult situations or people if they share experiences, successes, and failures. Time and again it turns out that a person who has exhibited difficult behavior at one branch or one public desk, has done the same thing at another branch or desk. If the staff talks to one another, collective approaches can be devised. Communication via the e-mail system is also crucial to protecting the staff and the public via the legal system. See the section on TEMPORARY RESTRAINING ORDERS for more information about this.

MAKING THE BASIC RULES WORK

1. Don't ignore problems; they rarely go away.

2. Listen carefully and assess the situation.

3. Maintain a calm, non-judgmental attitude.

4. Repeat the problem back to the person until you both agree on what the problem is.

5. When you understand what the problem is, take action, if you can, to resolve it.

6. Explain your position in firm, unambiguous language.

7. Avoid using a loud voice, or words that are moralizing or condescending.

8. State consequences.

9. Use teamwork.

10. Call outside help if necessary.

11. Communicate with your colleagues.

SPECIFIC COPING TECHNIQUES

1. The following pages describe specific coping techniques for handling various inappropriate behaviors.

2. The behaviors or problems are listed in alphabetical order.

3. Each subject starts with a box like this one, which gives a basic summary of what to do.

4. The summary is followed by more detailed explanation and discussion.

5. Three other Santa Cruz Library System Manuals are cited: the *Public Services Manual*, which contains all the Library System's policies and a lot of other information besides, the *Branch Emergency Plan*, which has instructions for handling injuries, illness, and disasters of nature, and the Blue Book, which describes the procedures and policies associated with the automation system.

Each of these manuals is available at your Branch and/or on the Staff Intranet.

Four Important Definitions

The Person in Charge is the senior person in the Branch at any given time, unless (at Central) someone else is designated on the schedule. In a smaller Branch, the Person in Charge is usually the Branch Manager, but can be who ever the Branch Manager designates.

The Person in Charge has an absolute obligation to stop doing whatever she or he is doing and cope with a problem situation if another staff person requests it.

> Be polite but firm: "I am sorry, but I must leave you to handle a problem which has just come up. So-and-so will help you in a minute [or] I will be back as soon as I can."

Law Enforcement is a single term for either the city police of Santa Cruz, Capitola, or Scotts Valley, or the Sheriff's Department. All are reached from a single Dispatcher at 911.

However, in the City of Santa Cruz, the Santa Cruz Police can also be reached by dialing 9-911.

Community Backup is the person or persons (usually local merchants) with whom the Branch Manager of a facility in the unincorporated areas establishes a working security relationship. This is necessary because law enforcement response can be so slow when great distances must be traveled.

Incident Report Form: We use these forms to keep records of the problem situations which arise. They are good for collecting data on how often a difficult situation comes up, or the history of the Branch's encounters with a particularly troublesome problem. Do not fail to fill out an Incident Report. The City of Santa Cruz has special procedures for handling risk management issues. When an incident involves any one of the following things, fax the Incident Report to the Administration Office (420-5601) immediately, and send in the hard copy within 24 hours. Do not keep a copy at the Branch:

> Injury to a patron or staff member
>
> Damage to Library or patron property
>
> Need to call law enforcement

This applies to all Branches, no matter where they are located. The Administration Office will file the City forms if required, or will return the Incident Report for the Branch's file.

ANGRY OR IRATE PEOPLE

1. Remain calm. Do not give the appearance of being combative, but do not appear fearful either.

2. Listen attentively and nod appropriately.

3. Speak slowly, clearly, and in a moderate tone of voice.

4. Take immediate action if you can.

5. If you can't achieve a resolution to the problem, pass the patron on to your supervisor.

6. Avoid behaviors that typically annoy patrons. See the list at the end of this section.

Probably the problem situations encountered most frequently by Library staff are those involving people who are angry. The staff has developed the following basic rules, and some special techniques through long experience.

1. Remain calm. Do not give the appearance of being combative but do not appear fearful either.

2. Listen attentively and elicit as much information as you can about the complaint. Nod appropriately. Not only does this communicate attentiveness to the patron, but it may help you relax.

3. Be aware of how you are speaking. Speak slowly and clearly and if you are using a loud tone, lower your voice.

4. Be aware, also, that other library patrons are listening. What you say to the angry patron will be judged by people who are not involved. A demeanor of calm and reason keeps other listeners on the Library's side, and conveys information about Library policies.

5. When you understand what the problem is, take some immediate action. If the patron's complaint is legitimate, do something immediately to remedy the situation. For example, if a patron is complaining about a long wait for a Request, check to see where the patron stands on the list, give her/him this information, and say how many copies of the item we have purchased or leased.

6. If you can't achieve a satisfactory resolution to the problem, pass the patron on to your supervisor or to System Administration.

The Paraphrasing Technique

In many arguments, but especially those involving emotional issues, one of the problems is that the combatants don't listen to each other. One side is busy preparing her/his rebuttal while the other side is still speaking.

The paraphrasing technique is useful because it ensures that both sides really listen. They must in order to restate the other person's position.

1. As the angry patron states her/his problem, feed back the patron's own words by repeating what has been said (paraphrase).

2. Once you have paraphrased the patron's previous statement, secure confirmation from the patron that your paraphrase is an accurate restatement of what was said.

3. If the patron says your paraphrase was not accurate, try again until you get agreement. Or, ask the patron to restate the point. Paraphrase again until you have done so to the patron's satisfaction.

4. State the Library's position only when your paraphrasing has been accepted by the patron.

5. When the patron wants to speak again, she/he must accurately paraphrase you and receive your agreement before speaking.

Here's an example of what a staff person might say when dealing with a user who is angry about the time limit for using an internet terminal:

PATRON: I think it is outrageous that you are limiting my time at this terminal. I have as much right to use it as anybody else.

STAFF: You don't like our one-hour time limit for Internet use, is that what you're saying?

PATRON: Yes, that's right. And I don't understand why. I'm not done.

STAFF: Well, we have a one-hour limit on use of the internet terminals so that as many people as possible can use them. We only have six here at this

Branch and a lot of people need them. So we limit the time any one person can use them.

PATRON: But there isn't anybody waiting to use this terminal, so I shouldn't have to get off.

STAFF: You think you should be able to keep on using a terminal until somebody else wants it, right?

PATRON: Right. It's just going to stand here empty.

STAFF: We have our rule so that when someone comes in they see that a terminal is empty and they sign up to use it. If all the terminals are in use all the time people won't ask. So do you understand why we have the rule?

PATRON: I suppose so. But I still don't agree with it.

NOTE: Often, you are not going to be able to get a user to actually repeat back what you have said. The most important point is to get the user to agree that she/he understands that there are two points of view, one of which is yours. So you should *ask* the user if she/he understands, and if she/he doesn't, start again.

The Stand and Deliver Technique

Sometimes a patron is too angry for paraphrasing to work. The patron is furious, and wants a chance to express her/his rage to someone from the library. No staff person needs to listen to abusive or obscene language from a library user (see VERBAL ABUSE OF STAFF), but there is a technique for handling other people who are angry. We call this the "Stand and Deliver Technique" because the staff person stands there and the patron delivers his/her anger.

1. Remain calm. Do not give the appearance of being combative but do not appear fearful either.

2. Listen attentively and nod appropriately.

3. Don't attempt to respond to the patron. If you do, the patron will simply interrupt you. For the moment, just stand there nodding and murmuring affirmative sounds appropriately.

4. Eventually, the patron will talk her/himself out. When she/he does, state the library's position on the patron's problem.

5. Work hard to keep yourself from arguing with the patron; simply restate the library's policy over and over.

6. While remaining firm, try to find alternatives that will mitigate the situation without violating policy. Perhaps you can even ask the patron to help you think of acceptable alternatives.

7. If, after following these guidelines, the angry patron still will not let go, call the Person in Charge. If you are the Person in Charge, refer the patron to the Director of Libraries. Often angry people will respond more positively to "the boss."

Requests for Special Treatment

If the patron's complaint is not legitimate and she/he wants you to make a special exception for her/him, or alter established policy, you need to be firm. Explain the library's policy and show the patron a written copy of it if necessary.

A typical example of this kind of behavior is a patron who wants you to lend him/her a reference book to take out of the branch to copy at a cheaper copy shop, or to use at home overnight.

USER: Come on! You *know* me. I've been using this Branch for five years. I'm not going to *steal* it. Let me have it to take to Kinko's, and I promise I'll have it back by 5 P.M.

STAFF: I'm sorry, but I am really not able to do that. I know you wouldn't steal it, but if you have it out making copies the next patron who comes in can't use it.

USER: How about if I came back at closing time to pick it up and got it returned by the time you open in the morning?

STAFF :   Again, you can't guarantee that an emergency won't prevent you from returning it. Sorry, but we just can't allow you to take it out of the Library.

Staff Behaviors That Typically Annoy Patrons

While it is true that patrons can behave very badly, there are also certain behaviors by public desk works that can cause patron annoyance, and should consequently be avoided by staff at all costs:

- Embarrassing an adult in front of his or her children.
- Embarrassing a teenager in front of his or her peers (especially his, but girls don't respond well to this treatment either).
- Cold or marginally hostile demeanor, or simply failure ever to smile.
- Inability to make eye contact with the person being served.
- Continuing conversations with colleagues while waiting on a patron.
- Calling users by their first names when on personally acquainted.
- Talking in jargon, e.g., OCLC, LC, periodical, OPAC, interface, ISBN, monograph, serials, and so on.
- Calling anyone "honey" or "dear."
- Making users feel even sillier than they already do for asking a question.

BOOK COMPLAINTS AND QUESTIONS ABOUT LIBRARY MATERIALS

1. Use friendly questioning to establish the nature of the patron's concern.

2. If you do not feel you can handle a library materials question well, pass the patron on to your supervisor right away.

3. Make sure the patron knows the library has other materials in the subject area.

4. Explain that the professional staff selects materials on the basis of the Collection Development Plan and the Library Bill of Rights.

5. Ask the patron to fill out a Comment Form so that a senior librarian can respond.

Library staff members are very sensitive about issues concerning what we call "intellectual freedom:" attempts by members of the public, elected officials, or anyone else to censor the materials in the library. Therefore we sometimes respond defensively when anyone challenges a particular book or other item.

On the other hand, most people who raise questions about a book or other item don't think of themselves as censors and they don't believe in censorship. They simply don't like specific materials, and want to be able to tell somebody (i.e., a library staff person) about it.

Thus the staff's object in handling a question or complaint about library materials is to ensure that the individual has the opportunity to talk out what she/he thinks, that she/he knows the full range of materials the library offers in the subject area, and that she/he understands the library's procedures for selecting materials.

The outcome of a patron complaint may in the end be the person filling out a Library Materials Comment Form, but this should happen only after the staff person has worked to achieve the objectives above.

1. If an individual questions the selection of library materials (either a specific book or other item, or the policy in general), question her/him in a friendly and neutral way to establish the exact nature of the objection. Stay calm and remember that everyone has a right to an opinion.

   If you do not feel that you can handle this kind of situation effectively, pass the person on to your Branch Manager or the Person in Charge.

2. Make sure the individual knows that the library has other material in the subject area.

3. Explain that the professional library staff is responsible for selecting library materials, and that it uses a Collection Development Plan for this.

4. Explain that the basis of our policy is the Library Bill of Rights and the Freedom to View Statement of the American Library Association. The library's job

is to provide materials and information presenting all points of view on current and historical issues. This applies to both written documents and audiovisual materials.

> Copies of the Library Bill of Rights and the Freedom to View Statement are in the Public Services Manual. Each Branch Manager has a copy of the Collection Development Plan.

5. If the person persists in complaining about a specific item, ask her/him to fill out a Library Materials Comment Form. There is a copy of this form at the end of this Manual, or get one from your Supervisor/Branch Manager. Be sure that the form is filled out completely. If necessary, explain to the complaining patron that the staff does not respond to complaints about library materials without a written Comment Form.

6. Give the completed Library Materials Comment Form to your Branch Manager who will pass it on to the Assistant Director. One of the System Coordinators or the Assistant Director will telephone or write to the complainant.

Here's an example of one kind of complaint, with added information on how the staff handled it. It is a true story.

Man arrives at Central Branch Children's Room Desk and slaps down three books.

USER: I can't believe you have these kinds of books in your children's collections. Look at this [he picks one up]: *What Happens to a Hamburger*. And this: *About the Foods You Eat*. I have never seen anything more biased. These are encouraging children to kill animals. I don't think the library should have books like this!

STAFF: You object to these books being in the library collection, is that it?

USER :   I certainly do. And what is this, *The Natural Cook's First Book*? We ought to be training our children to eat vegetables instead of chicken and eggs and milk. I'm *serious*. I think the library is *criminal* to promote viewpoints which endanger health and the whole planet.

STAFF :   Actually, having a book on the shelves isn't promoting it. Our job is to provide information on all things, including different sets of beliefs. And I know we have some books on vegetarianism. Let's look in the catalog for them, shall we?

USER :   But it is wrong to teach children to disregard their own health.

STAFF :   The library has a policy for selecting books and all our materials. It is called the Library Bill of Rights, and it says that the library's job is to provide materials and information presenting all points of view on issues. I can give you a copy if you'd like to read it.

USER :   Well, that may be, but what I want to know is who bought *these* books. Did the person know any better?

STAFF :   The professional library staff selects all our materials, based on our Collection Development Plan, and on the Library Bill of Rights. If you want to know why the staff picked these *particular* books, you need to

fill out this form. Here's a copy of the form and also a copy of the
Library Bill of Rights.

USER: No, I don't *want* to do one of your forms. I just want you to know I
think it is outrageous to have books like these on the shelves for children. We should be teaching them what is healthy, not how to poison
their bodies. Here: I have a list of four books that would be much better for you to own.

STAFF: The staff will be interested to hear your comments on the books, and
whoever is responsible for that part of the collection will send you a
written response. But you do have to fill out the form if you want them
to consider your opinion. You do that, and I'll clip your suggestion list
to it.

OUTCOME:

The Youth Services Coordinator wrote the patron a letter explaining
that the library endeavors to present all sides on issues. She said that
she had reviewed the books he complained about, and that she was
satisfied that they fairly represented the view that chicken, eggs, milk,
and meats are part of a balanced diet.

She went on to point out two books at the Live Oak Branch (the user's
home branch) describing a vegetarian lifestyle. And she invited him to
suggest other titles for purchase, commenting that all four of the titles
he had listed were written for adults, rather than children.

THE LIBRARY MATERIALS RECONSIDERATION PROCESS:

The Branch Manager sends the Library Materials Comment Form on to the Assistant Director, who copies it for the Director, and sends it to the Youth Services
Coordinator, the Reference Coordinator, or to a selection librarian. Who is assigned
to handle the complaint depends on the subject of the material. The staff person
assigned tries to reach the patron by telephone to clarify the exact nature of the
complaint. A written response or a follow up to the phone call is mailed within two
weeks.

A patron who wishes to complain or comment further about a specific item:

1. Must write a letter to the Director of Libraries, who will review the documentation, and respond within two weeks.

2. May write an appeal of the Director of Libraries decision to the Chair of the
Library Joint Powers Board, who will schedule the matter on the agenda of the
next regular Board meeting. Part of the agenda consideration will be a report
from the staff.

PROBLEM SITUATION MANUAL
RECONSIDERATION OF LIBRARY MATERIALS

Reconsideration of Materials

An Extract from the Monroe (Indiana) County Public Library
Collection Policy Statement
April 1, 2002

The selection and de-selection of materials for the library is an on-going process, involving many different staff and many interactions with the community using the materials. Members of the community may have questions about the process or about selection of specific items. These questions are addressed as follows.

1. Questions concerning the process itself or the presence of a specific item in the collection should be answered by a selector. Often this discussion can clarify such areas as the scope and inclusiveness of the collection, the role of individual and parental responsibility in making personal choices form the general collection, and the availability of selection guides and professionals in finding appropriate materials for each individual.

2. Patrons may wish to suggest alternative materials and may need to know about the process of making "Suggestions for Purchase" (form attached).

3. Patrons may wish to know more about the basic policies that govern selection including the following:

   • Materials are not excluded because of the race or nationality or the social, political, or religious views of the authors or creators

   • Materials should present all points of view concerning problems and issue of our times; no materials should be proscribed or removed because of partisan or doctrinal disapproval

   • Materials should be chosen for value of interest, information and enlightenment of all the people of the community, including those whose are in minorities of this community

   • The scope of library materials is as broad as possible to allow for the maximum possibility of free expression and free access to ideas

   • The origin, age, background or viewpoint of a library user does not deny or abridge that person's right to full use of the library

   • In the case of children, the library supporters the right of the parent—and only the parent—to restrict his children—and only his children—from access to library materials and services. The library does not take on an "in local parentis" rule and it is the responsibility of each parent to advise and guide his own children.

4. Patrons may choose to ask for a formal review of specific materials. The patron is given a "Request for Reconsideration" form (form attached) and asked to fill this form out as completely as possible. When the form is returned to the library, it should go first to the Department Manager in the area where the material is held.

Request for Reconsideration of Library Materials
Monroe County Public Library*303 E. Kirkwood*Bloomington, IN 47408*812-349-3050

■■

Patron Name (*please print*) _____

Address: _____ Zip: _____

Phone Number: _____ Email: _____

Patron represents (*please circle one*): himself/herself

                                  Name of group or Organization _____

Author:_____

Title: _____

Media Type (*please circle one*):

Book   Magazine   Audio CD or   Videocassette   CDROM   Electronic   Other
                   Audiocassette   or DVD

1. **Why should the library reconsider this material?**

2. **For what age group would you recommend this material?**

3. **Is there anything good about this material?**

4. **Did you read/view the entire item?   If not, then what parts?**

5. **What would you like the Monroe County Public Library to do about this material?**

6. **What materials would you recommend to substitute and/or supplement the collection?**

Signature of Patron: _____

Date: _____

■■

Staff Member (*please print full name*):

Department: Date:

Library's Response (*please note on back or attach*) Date:

---

5. All members of [a special review committee comprised of the Department Manager, the Selector, and the Library Associate Director] will read, view, or listen to the material. Original reviews and other pertinent information will be researched.

6. The committee will meet to discuss and evaluate the material, and a response will be determined. A report of the committee's response will be sent to the person who submitted the "Request for Reconsideration" form.

CHATTY PEOPLE WHO DISTRACT STAFF

1. Be polite, but discourage long conversations.

2. Be direct in stating that you must do other work.

3. Help other staff members trapped in this situation by intervening if you can.

Chatty people are sometimes lonely people, and the staff should be tolerant of their behavior and needs.

Be polite, but discourage long irrelevant conversations with people.

If a person continues a lengthy conversation, politely explain that it is necessary to return to work or to help another library user.

EXAMPLE:

STAFF: Look, it's been fun talking with you, but I do have work to do for other people. Thanks for coming in.

Other staff members should be aware of situations like this, and intervene to help their colleague break up the conversation.

If there are two phone lines, try calling your trapped colleague.

CHILD ABUSE BY PARENTS OR CAREGIVERS

1. Intervene if you can to protect the child, but do not endanger yourself.

2. Try to distract the angry adult.

3. Try to get the name of the adult.

Incidents of adults (parents or other caregivers) physically abusing children in the library are surprisingly frequent. "Abuse" is defined as a physical act designed to hurt the child, including repetitive slapping, excessive spanking, and arm twisting.

Adults who abuse children are very angry. They could easily turn on a person who intervenes, and physically attack. Or, they could increase their attack on the child, or later blame the child for staff intervention.

Therefore, the objective in a library staff intervention has to be distracting the adult to bring the immediate abuse to a stop.

California law places the same requirements on library workers as teachers and child care workers: they must report cases of suspected (or observed) child abuse. Therefore, our Library System's policy is to document each observed case, to try to determine the name and address of the adult and the child, and to report cases to law enforcement.

1. If you observe an incident of child abuse, or suspect that one is occurring in the children's rest room, intervene to try to distract the adult, if you can do so safely.
2. Do not physically get between the adult and the child.
3. Use language which objectifies the situation, such as "We don't allow hitting in the library."
4. Do not use language which accuses the adult, such as "We don't allow child abuse in the library," or "You stop hitting that child."
5. Try to obtain the name and address of the adult.
6. Write down a description of the incident as quickly as possible and telephone law enforcement, notifying your Branch Manager that you are doing this.
7. Fill out and send an Incident Report, along with the Police Case Number, to Headquarters within 24 hours.
8. E-mail Branch Managers and Youth Services colleagues about the event.

CHILDREN LEFT UNATTENDED

1. Comfort a frightened child.
2. Attempt to locate the parent or caregiver.
3. If found, firmly explain the Library's "no-unattended" policy.
4. If the Library is closing, follow procedures in your Branch's Emergency Plan.

Children separated from or left unattended by their parents are often frightened and may be crying. They should be comforted by staff.

If it is determined that a child is lost or has been left unattended, take the child to the Young People's room staff at Central or to the Branch Manager at other Branches. Notify the Person in Charge.

The Young People's room staff or Branch Manager should try to identify or locate the parents or responsible person. If the Branch has one, use the telephone microphone to call for the parent or caregiver, or at a smaller Branch call out in a loud voice. When the person is located, firmly explain the library's policy on unattended children.

> *Children Under 9 Must Be Supervised by a Person 14 Years of Age or Older*

If the responsible adult cannot be found, call law enforcement, using the procedures in the Branch's Emergency Manual.

If the library is closing and the parents or responsible adults have not returned for their child, or cannot be contacted, the Person in Charge should follow the procedure outlined in the Branch's Emergency Manual.

Staff should remain with the child until appropriate arrangements have been made.

Under no circumstances should a staff member drive the child home.

If the child is taken to another place (the Fire Station, the Police Station, etc.), leave a note on the door stating where and at what time the child was taken.

If the child is taken to another place, fill out an Incident Report, and send it to the Admin Office within 24 hours.

Policy on Unattended, Lost or Missing Children
Duluth (Minnesota) Public Library

Statement of Purpose

It is the intention of this policy to enlist the cooperation of parents and other adults responsible for children to ensure that the Duluth Public Library provides a safe and pleasant experience for all who use it. This policy is to be implemented when children are lost, frightened, stranded or otherwise need assistance because they are alone.

Policy Statement

Children age seven and under may not be left alone in the Library. Parents/ caregivers are responsible for children's behavior.

Children Left Unattended During Open Hours

If it is determined that a child is lost or left unattended, a staff member should try to identify and locate the parent/caregiver, according to the following procedure:

a. Children left unattended are often frightened and crying and should be reassured by staff.

b. Walk around the area with the child, looking for the parent/caregiver and informally asking for assistance. Often other people in the area can provide information.

c. Page the child's parent/caregiver, using his/her name, if known, or the child's name, if known. If no name is available, describe the child's physical appearance. Repeat the page as needed. A sample page is:

> *May I have your attention please. Will Johnn's mother please come to the Children's Area? Johnny is wearing red overalls and a Power Rangers turtleneck.*

d. When an adult is located, gently remind him/her about the Library policy on unattended children. For example, "Your child is scared. The Library thinks it's important that an adult stay with a child under age 8."

e. If the parent/caregiver is not found in the building, a staff member should stay with the child until someone can be located, through searching the computer database, phone book, city directory, etc.

f. If, after making an attempt, the parent/caregiver has not been located the staff member will call the police (9-911). Explain to the child that no-one is in trouble but that we want to make sure the child gets home safely.

g. Under no circumstances will a staff member take the child out of the building.

Child Left Unattended at Closing

a. Check through the building and page the child's parent/caregiver. Repeat the page as needed.

b. If the parent/caregiver is not in the building, *two* staff members should stay with the child until someone can be located. Normal efforts to locate parents, relatives, neighbors/ family friends, etc. should be made, using information from the child. The computer database, phone book and a city directory may be used if necessary.

c. If, after making an attempt, the parent or another responsible adult has not been located, call the police (9-911). Explain to the child that no-one is in trouble but that we want to make sure the child gets home safely.

d. Under no circumstances will a staff member take the child out of the building.

Child Reported Lost or Missing

If a parent/caregiver reports a child missing, staff will follow this procedure:

a. Obtain the name, age and description of child.

b. Page staff to request their assistance in locaing the child, or page the child, depending on his/her age. Provide a name and/or description of the child. Watch exits.

c. Check all areas thoroughly, including bathrooms, offices and the elevator.

d. Check outside the Library.

e. Call the police (9-911) if unable to locate the child.

f. If the child is found and the staff was paged, make an announcement that the child has been found.

Timelines and actions may vary with the maturity of the child, the time of year, the weather and staff availability. The goal is to be helpful and to keep library patrons safe.

Adopted May 8, 1996
Duluth (MN) Public Library Board

CONFIDENTIALITY OF LIBRARY RECORDS

1. All records of library use are confidential.

2. Do not give any member of the public or government official information about what a library user has checked out or whether she/he has used the Internet.

3. If a law enforcement officer presents you with identification and a subpoena or other court order, refer him/her to the Director of Libraries.

4. See below for exceptions to these rules for adults, parents, and children.

California law (Public Records Act, Government Code Title 1, Division 7, Chapter 3.5, Sections 6254, 6254.5, 6255, and 6267) guarantees the confidentiality of all public library records. This means that staff may not give information about what a library client has checked out, asked the Reference staff, or whether s/he has ever signed up for Internet use.

There are only two circumstances in which this information may be given:

1. If a law enforcement officer secures an order from the court requiring the Library System to give information about a person's library use.

   When a law enforcement officer presents the court order, immediately refer him/her to the Director of Libraries, who will refer the order to the City Attorney for validation.

2. If an adult has the borrower card of his/her child, and wishes to know what the child has checked out, staff may give the information. Or, if an adult has the borrower card of her/his spouse and wishes to pick up the spouse's request item(s), staff may give the item(s). But the staff may not give other information about the spouse's account.

Our assumption is that the adult would not have the borrower card without permission. We acknowledge that this is somewhat shaky logic, but difficult encounters with parents "just trying to find out what my child has checked out so I can find it and return it" have led us to conclude that flexibility leads to better service.

This policy does *not* apply to giving information about Internet use or reference questions.

DISRUPTIVE BEHAVIOR

1. Approach the person(s) (adult, young adult, or child) and tell him/her that his/her behavior is inappropriate.

2. Be polite, be specific, and state consequences.

   "When you talk loudly, it disturbs other people. Please lower your voices or you will have to leave the Library."

3. Get backup from other staff if you have trouble.

4. If a second warning doesn't work, ask the patron to leave.

5. If the person won't leave, call law enforcement.

"Disruptive behavior" is usually not physically threatening, but is nonetheless disturbing to other library users. It can occur either inside or outside the library. Examples include a person audibly cursing, two people having a loud argument, a group of teenagers engaging in horseplay, or children pounding on the windows from outside the building.

Other users are not always quick to report disruptive people, so be alert to signs that a patron behaving inappropriately is disturbing other people. The signs include:

- Patrons moving away from another patron.
- Patrons staring at another patron.
- Patrons looking at staff members.

1. If a patron disrupts library users or staff (whether intentionally or not), approach the person, explain that the behavior is inappropriate in the library and ask the patron to stop at once. Explain what the patron is doing which is disruptive, and say what the consequences will be if she/he does not stop.

   "When you curse out loud like that, it really bothers other people. Is there something I can help you with? Please do stop swearing, or you will have to leave the library."

2. Groups of children who become noisy should be told in a firm, but nice way that their behavior is inappropriate in a library and is disturbing to others.

   "Kids, when you run up and down the stack aisles like that, it frightens older people, and it is dangerous. Please stop it right now. If you don't, I'll have to ask you to leave."

3. Groups of teenagers who are acting out need to be handled calmly but firmly. Be direct and concrete about what they are doing which disturbs other people. Do not show fear or allow yourself to be sidetracked or intimidated. Never physically touch a young person. Resist the temptation to isolate the group's leader and embarrass him or her.

4. If the group or person continues to be disruptive, give a second warning, restating the consequences. Get backup from a co-worker.

5. If you are not the Person in Charge, tell that person what is going on.

6. If the second warning is not effective, ask the person or group to leave the library. If they refuse, explain that you will call law enforcement. Then do it if necessary.

7. Write an Incident Report for your Branch's file. If a person is injured, property is damaged, or law enforcement is called, send the Incident Report to the Central Office within 24 hours.

Added Instructions for Handling Disruptive Children

1. When a parent or other caregiver is present, but fails to correct disruptive behavior by a child, don't hesitate to speak directly to the child yourself. Try to avoid physically touching a child, except of course to protect the child's safety.

2. If the behavior continues, tell the parent that his/her child is disturbing others, and that the library holds parents responsible for the behavior of their children. Do not let yourself be intimidated by a parent who believes you have misjudged or unfairly "disciplined" her/his child. If the parent complains about your treatment, refer her/him to your supervisor, or ask the parent to write out the complaint. Tell the parent that your supervisor will respond by telephone or in writing.

3. Parent use of the library as a temporary baby-sitting service should be dealt with firmly. Tell parents that the library does not provide such a service and cannot be responsible for their children. Point out the library's posted rule that children under 9 must be supervised by a person 14 years of age or older.

4. Programs for children (story hours and the like) inevitably draw lots of kids who are excited and thus noisy. Should an adult patron complain, respond sympathetically, explain the circumstances, and try to be specific about when things might calm down.

   "Yes, I know it is noisy right now. They are having a special mask-making program in the Children's Room, and everyone is very excited. It should be over in another half hour. We are trying to keep a lid on, but you know how kids are."

Added Instructions for Handling Groups of Young Adults

1. We encourage pre-teens and teenagers to use the library and its resources for working on school and other projects. And we understand that young people are often most comfortable working in groups. This does not mean, however, that young adults can interfere with other people's ability to use the library.

2. When we have a group of "regulars" who are causing or continue to cause problems, the Branch Manager or the Branch's Youth Services Librarian should try contacting the appropriate school for help in talking to the youngsters or reaching parents.

3. Taking Polaroid pictures of rowdy kids is a useful means for identifying them to school officials.

See also CHILDREN LEFT UNATTENDED
      DRUNKENNESS
      EMOTIONALLY/MENTALLY DISTURBED PATRON

DRUG & CHEMICAL DEPENDENCY PROBLEMS

1. Get backup from another staff person if you can.

2. Ask disruptive people to leave the Library.

3. Do not make the person feel threatened by standing close to him/her, and do not touch the person.

4. Call law enforcement for assistance.

Staff Witnessing the Sale or Use of Illegal Drugs Are Required to Notify Law Enforcement at Once.

It is not always obvious whether a person who is acting strangely is under the influence of drugs or suffering from a more permanent psychological problem. Whatever the case, if the person is interfering with other people's right to use the library by being disruptive, he/she must be asked to leave.

1. If you need help in dealing with an individual, get backup from a co-worker. At a larger Branch, consult with the Person in Charge. If you are on your own at a smaller Branch, be cautious in your approach; solicit help from other patrons if this seems appropriate.

2. Be careful not to make the patron feel threatened, as this will only make the situation worse. Do not touch him or her.

3. If the patron refuses to leave, or is incapable of leaving, call for law enforcement help.

4. A staff member or patron who witnesses the use or sale of illegal drugs should notify law enforcement at once.

5. Write an Incident Report for your Branch's file. If a person is injured, property is damaged, or law enforcement is called, send the Incident Report to the Administration Office within 24 hours.

DRUNKEN BEHAVIOR

1. Drunks can be dangerous and should be approached carefully.

2. Get backup help from a co-worker, and tell a disruptive drunk to leave the library.

3. If the person seems dangerous, call law enforcement immediately.

When a person smells of alcohol, staff members need to exercise judgment in deciding how to handle the situation. If the patron's behavior is not otherwise offensive, then there is no problem. If, on the other hand, the patron is noticeably intoxicated, loud, obnoxious, or if other patrons are complaining, action needs to be taken.

1. If you get into an argument (about an overdue book, or the length of wait on the Request List etc.) with a patron who smells of alcohol, be extra careful in your ANGRY OR IRATE PATRON handling technique. Probably the best approach is "Stand and Deliver"—don't argue, just listen. State the Library's point, and remember that the patron won't be so angry when she/he is sober.

2. People who are obviously drunk can be dangerous and should be approached carefully.

3. If the person seems dangerous, call law enforcement immediately. Don't worry about providing warning.

4. Get back-up help from co-workers and ask the individual to leave the building, because "Your behavior is inappropriate in the library."

5. If the individual refuses to leave, warn the individual that the police will be called.

6. If the problem persists and the individual will not leave, or is unable to leave, call law enforcement.

7. In the City of Santa Cruz, it is illegal to carry open bottles of alcohol.

8. Write an Incident Report for your Branch's file. If a person is injured, property is damaged, or law enforcement is called, send the Incident Report to the Administration Office within 24 hours.

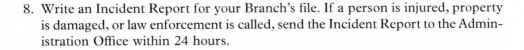

EATING OR DRINKING IN THE LIBRARY

1. Explain the rule against eating or drinking inside the Library.
2. Tell the person where they can eat or drink.

If a person is consuming food or beverages in the Library, or has an open container, approach the individual and explain the Library's policy. Suggest that the person finish the food or drink outside or in the lobby. If the person doesn't stop, ask him or her to leave the Library.

> "Excuse me, Sir. The Library has an absolute rule against eating or drinking inside the building. You will need to take that to the lobby or outside right now to finish it. Thanks."

This is the kind of situation that on a bad day can escalate into a difficult encounter. Be polite, stay calm, and be flexible. Coffee, soft drinks, and alcohol get spilled and mess up the rugs, tables, and library materials. Donuts and other messy food can do the same thing, and also attract bugs, which you might want to point out to the patron. The rule was written to prevent accidents with these kinds of food and drink. But a candy bar is not worth fussing about. The Common Sense Rule applies.

EMOTIONALLY OR MENTALLY ABERRANT BEHAVIOR

1. Use a firm, commanding voice to explain the library's rules and ask the person to desist or leave.
2. Do not corner or touch the person. Leave the person space to exit the building.
3. Get backup from co-workers.
4. Call for law enforcement help if the person will not leave.

Dealing with patrons who act or talk irrationally can be difficult. If the behavior is not disturbing to others, it should be ignored. Sometimes emotionally disturbed people are library regulars about whom the staff has information (name of the caseworker, address of sheltered living situation, etc.). Occasionally, the Branch Manager may feel that it would be more productive to call the caseworker than to involve the police. This is a Common Sense Rule situation. Provided the staff and public are not endangered, the Branch Manager should use her/his judgment in deciding who it would be best to call for help. If, on the other hand, the unusual behavior is disruptive, then the staff must act decisively.

1. Take a firm, consistent stand and speak in a commanding voice, explaining the library's rules and that, "Your behavior is disturbing to others and inappropriate in the library."

2. However, do not corner or touch the individual. Give the patron enough room to leave the building easily without feeling threatened.

3. If necessary, keep repeating your statement about appropriate behavior over and over.

4. If you are having difficulty dealing with the individual, call for help from co-workers and (in a larger Branch) let the Person in Charge know you are having trouble.

5. If the disturbance continues and the individual will not respond or is physically threatening to him/herself, other people or staff, call law enforcement immediately.

6. Write an Incident Report for your Branch's file. If a person is injured, property is damaged, or law enforcement is called, send the Incident Report to the Administration Office within 24 hours.

7. Send a System-wide message outlining the event and describing the person so that other staff will be alerted to a potential problem.

FIGHTS, PHYSICAL OR VERBAL

1. Tell other patrons to stand back.
2. Tell the combatants to stop immediately, or leave the library.
3. If they do not stop, call law enforcement.

One of the Library System's most famous stories about a fight between patrons involved the morning edition of the *Wall Street Journal*. A branch regular, known for his otherwise quiet and polite demeanor, became furious when another patron got to the paper first. He snatched the *Journal* out of the other man's hands, the other guy snatched back, and eventually they came to blows. The Branch Manager intervened, and ordered them to desist, which fortunately they did. In the end, they were persuaded to share. These were adults, not kindergartners.

The staff's *first objective in a physical confrontation between patrons is to protect the safety of other library users and staff.* This may not be easy, because other patrons may want to intervene. But if the person who intervenes is hurt, the Library could face serious liability problems.

1. In a very firm voice, order other patrons to stand back and not intervene.
2. Try to get the attention of the combatants. Order them to stop fighting immediately, or leave.
3. Do not endanger yourself by intervening physically.
4. When the fighting stops, warn the combatants that their behavior is totally inappropriate to the library, and that if it ever occurs again, the staff will get court orders forbidding them to come in to the library.
5. Call for law enforcement assistance if the fighting does not cease, or continues outside the building. Be prepared to give the police physical descriptions of the combatants.
6. Fill out an Incident Report, and send it to the Administration Office if law enforcement is called.

Treat verbal confrontations between patrons in the same way.

INTERNET POLICY COMPLAINTS OR QUESTIONS

1. Remember that everyone has a right to question or complain.
2. Use paraphrasing to find out what the question or complaint is really about.
3. Show the person the Library System's posted Internet Access Policy.
4. Refer the person to your Branch Manager or someone higher up if you can't satisfy them.

User access to the Internet has provided a whole new area of patron complaints and questions. The vast majority fall into two categories:

- People who complain or object to the Library System's rules for Internet use, especially the time limits.
- People who express their fear that other people, especially children, will be exposed to pornography or other harmful matter.

Handling Use Rule Complaints

1. Listen to the patron's complaint, paraphrasing as necessary.
2. Explain the Library's rules and the reasons for them:

   We limit length of use so as to provide maximum access for all library users. The Library's Internet access computers are a free service provided to the public and must be available to everyone.

   Except for viewing sexually graphic materials (see the next paragraph) we don't limit or censor how patrons use the Internet. E-mail is also information and so are games.

   Sexually graphic materials and images ("pornography") are protected by the First Amendment to the Constitution of the United States, so we do not filter our Internet access. But viewing sexually graphic sites is best done in private. The Library is a public space. Therefore, viewing sexually graphic Internet sites in the Library is inappropriate.
3. If a user wishes to complain further about use rules, encourage him or her to write a letter to the Director of Libraries.

Handling Expressed Fears about Access to Pornography and Other "Harmful" Matter

1. Listen to the patron's complaint, paraphrasing as necessary.
2. Explain the Library's policies and the reasons for them:

   The Library policy regarding the Internet was affirmed by the Library Joint Powers Board in October 1999, and posted in compliance with State law in January, 2000.

   The Library regards the Internet as an information resource like any other: books, videos, tapes, etc. It does not distinguish or discriminate on the basis of the age in providing access to information resources. Although children and adults have different information needs, and the Library's services for the two age groups are organized differently to meet them, we do not deny access to any collection or resource on the basis of age.

   Just as adults have the right to pick what they read and view, it is the responsibility of parents to decide what their children may read or view. The Library makes substantial efforts to help parents and caregivers make these decisions.

   The Library does not filter the Internet because filters do not work. These software programs filter out not only pornographic information, but health information as well. The First Amendment to the U.S. Constitution, which guarantees free expression and free access to information, is one of our most important national values.

   For these reasons, the Library Joint Powers Authority Board voted at its October 2003 meeting to *not* comply with the Child Internet Protection Act, which requires filtering if a library wishes to qualify for certain federal funds.

3. Encourage the person to write a letter to the Director of Libraries if she or he persists in complaining.

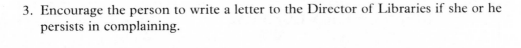

> # INTERNET USE PROBLEMS
>
> 1. Tell a user who complains loudly about the time limit on Internet use the reason for the rule.
> 2. Tell a user viewing a pornographic site to stop immediately.
> 3. If either inappropriate behavior continues, ask the user to leave the library.

The majority of Internet use problems involve patrons who don't want to abide by the One Hour rule, or those who want to view sexually graphic sites.

Handling Time Problems

1. The Library has installed software at most Branches that limits users to one hour on the Internet. Users must present a borrower card to access the terminals. Some users don't want to abide by the rules, and complain loudly when their time is up.

2. Explain the reason for the rule: to ensure that all community residents have a chance to use the Internet. Tell users who say there is no waiting list that we need terminals to be free for walk-in patrons.

3. Suggest other places (Kinko's, Cruzio, etc.) where unlimited rental time on Internet terminals is available.

Handling Sex-Site Access

1. If another user reports that someone is viewing a sex site, or if you spot someone doing that, tell the person to stop immediately. Point out the Library's posted rule regarding viewing sexually graphic sites.

2. If necessary, tell the user that if he/she does it again his/her Internet privileges will be blocked at this Branch and all other Branches.

3. See the previous section, INTERNET POLICY COMPLAINTS/QUESTIONS for advice about how to handle the discussion with the user who reported the other person.

LIBRARY POLICY COMPLAINTS OR QUESTIONS

1. Remember that everyone has a right to question or complain.
2. Remain calm and non-judgmental.
3. Use paraphrasing to find out what the question or complaint is really about.
4. Take action if you can.
5. Refer the person to your Branch Manager or someone higher up if you can't satisfy them.

All library users have a right to question general library procedures and policies. When such situations arise, staff members should:

1. Remain calm and be receptive and non-judgmental.
2. Listen carefully to the patron's question or complaint, nodding appropriately.
3. Use paraphrasing to establish the exact nature of the complaint, and pause and think before responding.
4. Clearly explain the library's policy and show a written copy of it to the patron if necessary. Remember to explain *why* we have a particular policy.
5. If you don't know the answer, say so, and refer the patron to someone who does. Being frank about your ignorance is always better than trying to fake it.

   "I'm sorry, Mrs. Jones. I've never worked in the cataloging department, so I don't know all the different things which go into setting the processing cost for a lost book. But I know our Branch Manager, Susie Smith, does. She comes in at noon today and is working tonight. May I ask her to call you?"
6. In explaining policy, it is nice if all staff takes grammatical responsibility for the library's policies. That is, try to refer to "we" rather than "they."
7. Follow through with action, trying to find alternatives if possible.
8. If necessary, refer the patron to another worker or to the Person in Charge.
9. If the person is still not satisfied, refer her/him to the Branch Manager, the appropriate Coordinator, the Assistant Director, or the Director.

Here's an example of what a staff person might say when dealing with a user who is angry about the staff's refusal to give him his wife's Request books without her borrower card:

USER: I don't get it. We are *married!* We live together and have for a lot of years! All I want to do is pick up the book she got notified is waiting for her.

STAFF: Do you have her borrower card or the notice she got?

USER: No. I have my own card and I just want to pick up my wife's book. Look, we even have the same name. Does your computer show addresses, because we live at the same place too.

STAFF: Here's the situation. California Law requires that all library records be kept confidential. That means that we can't check out an item to somebody besides the person who requested it, because that would be telling the person what the other person was borrowing. We can do it if we know you have permission—if you have brought her borrower card or the notice she got in the mail or the e-mail. Without those things, we can't. It's the law.

USER: I don't believe that. Even for people in the same family? Where is this law? I want to read it.

STAFF: It's in the California Public Records Act. I will get you a copy off the Library's Web Page.

For additional guidelines, see ANGRY OR IRATE PATRON

LOST CHILD IN THE LIBRARY

1. Use the telephone microphone system or other means to announce that a child is missing, briefly describing the child.

2. Deploy staff to assist in search.

3. If the child is not found within a reasonable time, call law enforcement.

4. If the child is located, use the telephone microphone or other means to announce success.

MISSING POSSESSIONS, STOLEN WALLETS, ETC.

1. Ask the user who reports a stolen item to retrace his/her steps within the building, thoroughly searching the building both inside and out.

2. If the item isn't found, urge the person to file a law enforcement report.

3. Get the name, address, and phone number of the person so that she/he can be contacted if the item turns up.

The Library System is not responsible for the personal property that patrons bring into our facilities. This not only includes purses, wallets, jackets, book bags, and lunch boxes, but the backpacks and duffels that may constitute all the worldly goods of a street person.

We encourage people to be careful of their possessions, and to not leave them unattended on tables, in carrels, or on the floor by a chair.

People do this anyway, of course, and consequently come to the staff to report that personal property is missing or stolen:

1. Ask the person if the item could have been misplaced or left somewhere else. If not, suggest that she/he retrace her/his steps within the building.
2. If the item is not found, suggest that the person search the building inside and out, looking in all the waste baskets, outdoor trash receptacles, landscaping areas, etc.
3. Urge the person to call law enforcement if the item is not found.
4. The staff member should take the name and telephone number of the patron and give it to the Branch Office in case the bag or other item is eventually located.
5. Write an Incident Report for your Branch's file. If a person is injured, property is damaged, or law enforcement is called, send the Incident Report to the Administration Office within 24 hours.

OBSCENE PHONE CALLS

1. Hang up. Do not listen.
2. Note the date and time of the call, and give the information to your supervisor.

There are people who get a thrill out of dialing a phone number and talking obscenely to whoever answers. Libraries, and their telephone reference operations, are easy targets for this kind of harassment.

The only way to handle the behavior is to not give the caller the satisfaction of listening. Just hang up. But do log the call, because if there is a sudden surge of obscene phone calls, we may decide to ask law enforcement to investigate.

Added Note:

If you receive an obscene phone call which is directed to you personally, in which the caller uses your name, your address, your car make or license number, or any other personal information about you, report this immediately to your supervisor, who will call the police.

PANHANDLERS OR SOLICITORS ON LIBRARY PROPERTY

1. If you see someone panhandling or soliciting on library property explain that it is illegal.

2. If necessary, warn the person a second time, saying you will call law enforcement.

3. If the person persists, warn a final time, and call law enforcement if necessary.

Panhandling and soliciting on library property are prohibited by the California Penal Code, #647(c).

Library property extends to the library side of the public sidewalk, and includes branch parking lots for facilities we own, but not the parking lots of leased spaces in shopping centers. Panhandling and soliciting is prohibited inside both owned and leased library facilities.

"Panhandling" is to accost someone and beg for something, usually money. "Soliciting" is to approach with a request or a plea. Although there are more exotic examples associated with this word, the soliciting we normally see in the library is by kids selling candy to benefit a school project, or the like.

1. If you witness a violation, explain the law to the offender.

2. If the problem persists, warn the person a second time.

3. If the person continues, warn the person a third time, explaining that you will call law enforcement if she/he does not desist.

4. Take a Polaroid picture of the violator if you can.

5. Write an Incident Report for your Branch's file. If a person is injured, property is damaged, or law enforcement is called, send the Incident Report to the Administration Office within 24 hours.

PERSONAL POSSESSIONS LEFT IN THE LIBRARY

1. The Library may not be used as a free storage place for personal possessions such a back packs, plastic bags of clothing, etc.

2. Tag the item with a filled out PLEASE REMOVE notice.

3. Fill out an UNATTENDED ITEM form and leave it at the Reference Desk.

4. After two hours, remove the item to the Library trash area.

5. Leave the PLEASE REMOVE notice behind with a note of the removal time and the place to which the item was moved.

Street and homeless people occasionally leave their personal possessions in the Library while they go to other places. This is particularly true at the Central Branch. Back packs, plastic bags of clothing, suitcases, bedrolls, and similar items take up space in the Library, and can present a hazard to other users.

At the same time, it is important to distinguish between unattended personal items of this sort, and "lost and found" objects: the odd wallet, notebook, car keys, sunglasses, etc. that have been forgotten inadvertently.

Although the Library staff must treat people's personal possessions with respect, it is not our job to provide free storage space. Storage is available at the Homeless Services Center.

1. If a back pack or other bulky personal item is left unattended, keep an eye on it, and if, after one hour, the item has not been retrieved, use the UATTENDED ITEM form to evaluate the situation. If necessary, tag the item with a filled out PLEASE REMOVE slip. See copies of these forms below.

2. Put the UNATTENDED ITEM form at the Reference Desk.

3. If the item has not been retrieved two hours after tagging, remove the item and put it next to the Library's trash dumpster. Fill out the rest of the PLEASE REMOVE form, and leave it at the place where the item was located.

4. Lost and found items should be held at the Circulation Desk for thirty days.

Unattended Items

In-house Checklist

Date _____

Staff name(s) _____

Item left unattended _____

Where in library found _____

Why is it a problem? _____

_____ Obstruction/blocking pathway area

_____ Obstruction/blocking seating access

_____ Hygiene for sanitary problem

Other _____

Time observed _____ Time rechecked _____

Action taken _____

_____

_____

Have you or other staff seen/tagged this item

Before? _____ Yes _____ No _____ Don't Know

Do you know the patron's real name or the name

we use to describe him/her?

_____

PLEASE REMOVE THIS ITEM

The Library System regrets that it cannot store people's personal belongings.
If you need such storage, contact the Homeless Services Center
at 115 Coral Street in Santa Cruz.

This item has been unattended for at least an hour. If it is still here in two hours, it will be removed to the Library Trash Area at the rear of the building.

Date: _____

Time Now: _____

Deadline for Removal: _____

Time Item Removed: _____

Location Moved To: _____

PETS IN THE LIBRARY

1. Animals are not allowed in the library.

2. Seeing Eye or Hearing Dogs, or any animal clearly trained to assist Disabled Users, are exempted from this rule.

3. Insist that any other animals be removed immediately.

People may not bring pets of any kind into the library. This includes the lobbies of branches that have them. There are three reasons for this rule:

- Animals confronting one another inside a building can get into fights that are unpleasant for everyone.
- Excited animals can cause accidents and discomfort among older and younger patrons.
- Many people are allergic to animal hair or animal odors.

Seeing Eye or Hearing Dogs, or other animals clearly trained to assist a disabled user, are exempt from this rule.

If someone brings in a pet:

1. Ask the person to remove the animal immediately.

2. Suggest that dogs be tied outdoors, in a place where they will not frighten children (such as bicycle racks), *not* on the entrance step railings.

3. If appropriate, remind the person that local ordinance requires that all dogs be leashed.

4. If the person refuses to abide by the library rule say you will call law enforcement. Do so if necessary.

5. Write an Incident Report for your Branch's file. If a person is injured, property is damaged, or law enforcement is called, send the Incident Report to the Administrative Office within 24 hours.

See Also Your Branch's Emergency Plan for Information on Animal Bites and Animals in the Library.

SEXUAL DEVIANCY REPORTS BY PATRONS

1. The staff's first obligation is to the patron who reports she/he has been sexually harassed.

2. Treat the victim with respect, sensitivity, and compassion.

3. If the victim is a child, try to find the parent.

4. Get as much information about the incident as you can.

5. Telephone law enforcement.

6. If possible, send someone to photograph the perpetrator.

Most sexual deviancy reports by library patrons involve exposure, which is unpleasant but not dangerous. Other forms of deviancy, including staring and stalking, can be dangerous. Read SEXUAL HARASSMENT OF STAFF BY THE PUBLIC for more information about these behaviors.

The library staff member's first obligation is to treat the complaining patron with sensitivity, compassion, and respect. The second obligation is to call law enforcement. Follow the procedures below for all types of deviancy reports.

1. Ask where the incident occurred and whether the person is still in the library. If possible, get the victim to point out the perpetrator. Get another staff person to take a Polaroid picture of the perpretrator. You stay with the victim.

2. Call 911 for law enforcement help. Give your name and Branch address. Tell the Dispatcher there has been an incident of sexual harassment, and encourage the victim to speak directly to the Dispatcher.

3. If the victim is unwilling to speak to the Dispatcher, give all the information communicated by the victim:

   Location of the incident
   Description of the incident
   Description of the suspect.
   If the suspect has left, give the last known location and the direction of travel.

4. Follow any special instructions of the Dispatcher.

5. Get the name, address and telephone number of the victim.

6. Ask the victim to sit down in a quiet corner and write down as full and accurate a description of the suspect as possible. Concentrate on age, height, type of build, color and style of hair, clothes and any distinguishing marks or mannerisms.

7. Then ask the victim to write down exactly what happened, where it happened, and what was said.

8. Encourage the victim to await the arrival of law enforcement in order to answer any further questions.

9. Send an e-mail account of the incident, including a description of the perpetrator to All Branch Managers. Branch Managers should share this information with their staffs.

10. Write an Incident Report and send it to the Administrative Office within 24 hours.

Added Instructions When the Victim Is a Child

1. If a child reports to you that she/he has been sexually harassed or approached, remember you have two obligations: to meet the immediate needs of the child, and to telephone law enforcement.

2. The child may be confused, frightened, or very upset. You act calmly, seeking to reassure and comfort the child.

3. Ask the child where the incident occurred, whether the person is still in the library and if the child's parent is there.

3. Send someone to find the child's parent. You stay with the child.

4. See if you can get the child to point out the perpetrator to you, and ask another staff person to take a Polaroid picture of him.

5. Describe to the parent what has happened, and say that you are obligated to report such incidents to law enforcement, which you are going to call right now.

   The parent will probably be upset too. Treat the parent with calmness. Try to take the parent and child into a quiet area, such as an office.

6. Call 911 for law enforcement assistance. Give your name and Branch address, say there has been an incident of sexual harassment involving a child, and give all the information communicated by the victim, as above.

7. Get the name, address and telephone number of the child.

8. If the child's parent is not present, contact him/her by phone to report the incident. Make sure there is a way for the child to get home safely. Law enforcement can help with this.

SEXUAL HARASSMENT OF STAFF BY CO-WORKERS

1. You have a right to work in an environment free of sexual harassment by your co-workers or supervisors, or by volunteers.

2. Tell the person who you believe is harassing you that you find the behavior inappropriate, and request that the person stop.

3. If the inappropriate behavior recurs, report it immediately to your supervisor or another manager.

The City of Santa Cruz has a Discriminatory Harassment Policy aimed at maintaining an employment environment free of harassment. "Harassment" is an action which has the effect of discriminating against individuals on the basis of race, religious creed, color, national origin, gender, and other factors. This Policy is set forth in Administrative Procedure Order Section II, #1A. All employees are encouraged to read it. It includes a procedure for investigating and resolving complaints of discriminatory harassment.

> *Sexual harassment is defined as unwanted sexual advances, or visual, verbal, or physical conduct of a sexual nature. This definition includes gender-based harassment of a person of the same sex as the harasser.*

Here are some of the behaviors:

- Unwanted sexual advances.
- Offering employment benefits in exchange for sexual favors.
- Making or threatening reprisals after a negative response to sexual advances.
- Visual conduct: leering, making sexual gestures, displaying sexually suggestive objects or pictures, cartoons or posters.
- Verbal conduct: making or using derogatory comments, epithets, slurs, and jokes.
- Verbal sexual advances or propositions.
- Verbal abuse of a sexual nature, graphic verbal commentaries about an individual's body, sexually degrading words used to describe an individual, suggestive or obscene letters, notes, invitations, or e-mail.
- Physical conduct: touching, assault, impeding or blocking movements.

The reality is that different people perceive comments, statements, jokes, and actions in different ways. What is funny to some employees is offensive to others. A remark intended as a casual compliment may be received as inappropriate harassment.

Supervisors who approach junior staff with requests for dates or other personal attentions are exploiting their position of authority. They may place the junior person in the position of being unable to respond negatively to the request, for fear of work-related reprisal.

Sexual approaches by a supervisor are absolutely inappropriate management behavior, and are subject to disciplinary action.

Here are some sensible rules for conduct by library workers:

1. If a co-worker or a supervisor makes sexually oriented jokes or comments to you which you consider offensive, tell the person. Say, "I think that remark is inappropriate. Please do not say things like that to me."

2. If the person persists, report the matter to your supervisor. *It is very important that you do this; we cannot create a harassment free environment if people are unwilling to speak out or complain.*

3. If the persisting person is your supervisor, report the behavior to her/his supervisor. Do this immediately. You will be protected. If you feel the supervisor will not handle the matter appropriately, report it directly to the Personnel Department. *Sexually harassing behavior by a manager is inappropriate, and subject to discipline. It cannot be investigated and stopped if it is not reported.*

4. It is absolutely forbidden to use the Library's or the City's electronic mail system for personal use, including messages with sexual content.

5. As a worker or a supervisor, do not comment, joke, or discuss matters with sexual implications (such as dress and appearance) with co-workers. The simplest way to avoid problems in this area is to talk about something else.

Examples of Inappropriate Remarks

"I like that blouse you're wearing."

"You look great in jeans."

"You look wonderful in blue."

"Curly hair like yours is such a turn on."

"I've always loved guys with mustaches."

SEXUAL HARASSMENT OF STAFF BY THE PUBLIC

1. *Exhibitionism [flashing]*: Walk away from the patron, and immediately call law enforcement.

2. *Following, Stalking, or Staring*: Tell the patron, "I think you are following me around [or staring at me]. It interferes with my work. Please stop it right now."

3. *Repetitive Requests for Sexually Oriented Materials or Information:* After the second request, say, "We gave you that information before. I am going to write it down for you, so you won't need to ask again."

4. *Unwelcome Requests for Dates*: Say, "No, I've told you, I will not go out with you. Please do not ask me again. If you keep bothering me, I will call the police."

These four examples are the most common ways staff are sexually harassed by patrons, but not the only ones. There are three rules to remember in handling sexual harassment:

1. Do not give the harasser the satisfaction of making you visibly upset. No matter how angry, embarrassed, or offended you are by the behavior, treat it calmly.

2. Be direct and clear in the limits you set. In cases 2, 3, and 4 above, it is important for the staff person to say what the boundaries of interaction are, and stick to them.

3. You have a right to work in a place in which you are not subjected to sexual harassment by the public or your co-workers.

Exhibitionism

People, usually men, with this sexual pathology are very rarely dangerous. The purpose of their action is to get attention for themselves. Exhibitionism is illegal, and should be treated as a crime.

1. Walk away from the perpetrator.

2. Telephone law enforcement and request assistance.

3. Immediately write a description of the perpetrator.

4. If you can, photograph the perpetrator with a Polaroid camera, or ask a co-worker to do this.

5. Send e-mail to all Branch Managers describing the incident and perpetrator. Branch Managers should tell their staffs.

6. Fill out an Incident Report and send it to the Administrative Office within 24 hours.

Following, Stalking, or Staring

This harassment technique is harder to handle because it looks innocent. In fact, however, it is potentially dangerous, as the increasing number of stalking cases reported in the media attests.

1. If you notice, for the second day (second shift, or whatever), that a patron is staring at you, or following you, write it down, as well as the previous incident. Also write a description of the patron.
2. Tell your supervisor if you have one.
3. Ask a co-worker to use a Polaroid to photograph the patron.
4. Try moving to a different work station if you can.
5. If the harassing behavior continues, with your supervisor, confront the patron. Either you or your supervisor can do the talking. Use direct language, stating what you believe to be the facts, and what you want the patron to do. The object is to convey to the patron that you and your supervisor mean business; sexually harassing behavior will not be tolerated.

STAFF: I think you are staring at me [or following me]. This interferes with my work. Please stop it immediately, or you will have to leave the library. Please move to another place to sit.

PATRON: What? I'm not staring at you! What are you talking about?

STAFF: Good. Then you won't mind moving to another place to sit. Please do that, right now.

6. If the harassing behavior continues, call for assistance from law enforcement.
7. Send e-mail to all Branch Managers describing the incident and perpetrator. Branch Managers should tell their staffs.
8. If law enforcement is called, file an Incident Report, sending it to the Administration Office within 24 hours.

Repetitive Requests for Sexually Oriented Materials or Information and Unwelcome Requests for Dates

See the summary box above. Also,

1. Make sure you report these incidents to both your supervisor and co-workers, so that other staff are alerted about the problem behavior by a patron.

SLEEPING PATRONS

Yakima Valley (Washington) Regional Library

Customer Relations Manual

A. Sleeping is not allowed in the library. Library users who simply doze off for a short period may be left alone. The library's regulation pertains to habitual sleepers or those who are noisy, sprawled out on the furniture, or generally disturbing other patrons.

B. Discretion should be used in approaching sleeping patrons. Do not physically touch or shake them. They may possibly swing out at you as you awaken them. Be sure to approach them from the front and at an arm's distance.

C. Tell the patron to remain awake.

D. Check back after approximately ten minutes. If the patron is still sleeping, wake him/her up and tell them to leave the building.

E. If the sleeping patron is drunk, will not leave, or is physically threatening, call the police.

SMELLY PEOPLE

1. Verify that the odor is so bad that it interferes with other people's ability to use the library.

2. Look for alternatives:

   Can the complaining patron move?

   Can the smelly patron move?

3. If not, ask the smelly patron to leave and not return until she/he has bathed and washed her/his clothes.

4. Give the patron a Shelter or Free Shower Flyer.

This is one of the most difficult situations staff can confront, particularly in areas where street people are frequent library users. Street people do not have easy access to bathing facilities or places where they can wash their clothes. This fact is not a reason to deny them access to the library. The only reason to deny them access is if they are so smelly that other people cannot use the library.

There are *other* kinds of odor problems which staff must sometimes handle. One is heavy use of perfume, which can offend other people. Another are people with severe environmental allergies, who complain that the library's air or the people around them are making them ill.

If a person's odor is so strong that it is offensive to staff or other library users (i.e., if it interferes with other people's ability to use the library), the Branch Manager or the Person in Charge should:

1. Verify the situation for her/himself. "So strong" means that it is literally nauseating to be near the person.

2. If another person has complained, ask the complainant if she/he is willing to agree to back the staff should a formal (i.e., police) complaint be necessary.

   If the person is not willing, evaluate whether the situation is worth pursuing anyway.

   > Can the complainant move?

   > Can the smelly person be asked to move?

3. If in your judgment the person must be asked to leave the library, quietly and politely do so, asking the person not to return until he/she has cleaned her/himself.

EXAMPLE: "Excuse me, Sir/Ma'am. I am sorry to say that the way you smell means other people cannot use the library. So I must ask you to leave right now. You can come back as soon as you have bathed and washed your clothes. Here is flyer for a place which offers free showers."

4. If the person objects, call law enforcement.

5. In the case of a person who smells offensive due to excessive perfume, follow the same procedures, but drop the statement about bathing and washing clothes.

6. Write an Incident Report for your Branch's file. If a person is injured, property is damaged, or law enforcement is called, send the Incident Report to the Administrative Office within 24 hours.

If a person complains that she/he has severe environmental allergies, the Branch Manager or Person in Charge should try to establish what can be done to mitigate the problem.

> Would opening the windows help?

> Can the person move?

> Would a fan help (but be careful about hazardous cords)?

It is important to convey sympathy to a user troubled by environmental allergies, and to attempt to make it possible for the person to use the public library. The Branch Manager might ask the patron whether she/he would find a volunteer helpful, and link the person with the Friends Office to find one.

However, the library's basic policy always applies: no one (even an allergic person) has the right to interfere with anyone else's right to use the library. There are limits on the modifications we can make.

SMOKING

1. It is illegal to smoke anything in any public building in Santa Cruz County.

2. Say to the violator:

   "I'm sorry, sir, but it is illegal to smoke inside any public building in Santa Cruz County. Will you please take that outside right now to put it out, or finish it there? Thanks."

3. If the violator refuses, call law enforcement.

STAFF NAMES

1. As public employees, library staff are required to give their full names to members of the public when requested.

2. If the person seems hostile, call your supervisor to talk with her/him.

3. If you suspect that the person's intentions are harassing or dangerous, follow the procedures in SEXUAL HARASMENT OF STAFF BY PUBLIC.

Staff often do not like to give their names to members of the public because they fear the person will retaliate. Since as a public employee you are *required* to give your name to anyone who asks for it, here are some ideas for handling the request:

1. Try giving your first name only.

2. In a hostile encounter, say to the user

   "If you want to complain about this library rule [transaction, whatever] or my work, let me call my supervisor who will be glad to talk with you."

   If you supervisor is not available, call a co-worker to fill the role.

3. If you suspect that the person's intent is to harass you, call your supervisor and follow the procedures in the SEXUAL HARASSMENT OF STAFF BY PUBLIC section of this manual.

4. If a person to whom you have given your name does harass you (for example by phoning you at your home) report the matter to your supervisor immediately and call law enforcement.

TEMPORARY RESTRAINING ORDERS AND 30 DAY COOLING OFF PERIODS

1. 30 Day Cooling Off Periods can be used to ban abusive or rule-breaking patrons as a warning about their behavior.

2. A TRO is a last resort action to protect the staff and public from an abusive person.

3. Document, document, document your encounters with difficult people. Use Incident Reports and e-mail.

4. Tell the Director of Libraries what you need; the Director is responsible for securing the temporary restraining order via the City Attorney.

Temporary Restraining Orders (TROs) are orders from the Superior Court forbidding a person to use a particular Library System branch or other facility. They are issued for a specific period of time, and can be made permanent only by going back to Court. The Director of Libraries works with the City Attorney to secure the order.

Securing a restraining order is a last resort course of action. By getting one, we are curtailing a person's fundamental First Amendment right to information. Therefore we do not take the action casually.

A first step in handling a very difficult patron is to *administratively ban* the person from using a Library facility for a specific period of time as a warning about their behavior. This is a "30 Day Cooling Off Period." The person may return after the period, but if s/he again violates our rules, we secure a Temporary Restraining Order banning them.

30 Day Cooling Off Periods

It is appropriate to ban a person via a 30 Day Cooling Off Period if the person is a repeated offender of the library's basic rules. Generally, in the recent past the person will have been asked to leave for the rest of that day, and will have been warned about his/her behavior. Examples are abusive people who threaten the staff and other patrons, shouters, Internet use rule violators, and the like. Acts of sexual deviancy such as harassment of staff or other patrons are also appropriate candidates for banning via a 30 Day Cooling Off Period.

Grosser acts of sexual deviancy (exhibitionism, harassment of children) involve law enforcement, and should go directly to the Temporary Restraining Order stage. *Criminal acts should be reported to law enforcement immediately without regard to prior warning.* 30 Day Cooling Off Period bans apply to single Branches in the Library System.

1. Fill out a three-part 30 DAY COOLING OFF PERIOD form (hereinafter 30DCOP form, see sample attached).

2. Give Part 1 of the 30DCOP form to the patron. Tell the patron that her/his behavior violates Library rules, that s/he must leave the Library immediately, and that s/he may not return for 30 days. Tell the patron s/he is banned from this Branch for this period, and the date on which s/he may return.

3. If Law Enforcement is involved in the situation, explain to the Officer what you are doing.

4. Tell the patron that if, when s/he returns, Library rules are again violated, the Library staff will secure a Temporary Restraining Order from the Courts banning him/her from Library use for a longer period.

5. Tell the patron that s/he has the right to appeal the banning rule to the Branch Manager within 24 hours. Give the patron the Branch Manager's name and office phone number. If you are the Branch Manager, tell the patron s/he may appeal to the Director of Libraries (or her designee) and give the Director's name and office phone number (420-5600).

6. File an Incident Report with the Branch Manager immediately, attaching Part 2 of the 30DCOP form. The Branch Manager should immediately fax the Incident Report to Library Administration.

7. Give Part 3 of the 30DCOP form to the most appropriate Public Desk.

8. Send email to other Branches reporting the incident and your action. Describe the patron as completely as possible. Branch Managers should be alert to abusive patrons transferring their actions to other libraries. However, a 30 Day order will not prohibit the patron from using another branch.

9. If the patron requests a hearing, the Branch Manager or Director of Libraries should hold it at the Branch within 24 hours of the request. Procedures for conduct of the hearing should be as fair as possible. State the rules at the beginning, e.g., length of time allowed for presentations (five minutes for each side would be adequate), no interruptions, etc. State the process. Then ask the Branch staff representative to state the staff case, ask the patron to state her/his case, summarize the two positions, and decide on a course of action.

Temporary Restraining Orders

If it is necessary to secure a Temporary Restraining Order against a repeat offender, follow this procedure:

1. If you have a documented situation (Incident Reports, Police Case Reports, internal e-mail messages) that you believe calls for a restraining order, the Branch Manager should write the Director of Libraries a memorandum and send it with the documentation. If the situation is an emergency, say so, and take whatever action is necessary to ensure swift action: an advance alert by e-mail, hand-carrying the documentation to Headquarters, faxing, etc.

2. The Director will immediately write the City Attorney a request for a TRO on behalf of the Library System, attaching the documentation to the memo.

3. The City Attorney will fill out the paperwork and file it with the Superior Court. Library staff may be contacted by the City Attorney to provide further information, sign documents, and provide other assistance.

4. The City Attorney will ask the Library staff to indicate whether we wish the restraining order to apply System-wide, to certain Branches, or to only one. Making this decision depends on having good information about where else the person has been troublesome.

5. Once the Superior Court has granted the TRO, it must be served on the person who is named within a certain number of days. This is the job of the County Sheriff's Department (not the City Police). Serving requires an address, of course, which we often don't have for street people. Therefore, it may well fall to the Library Staff to serve the order the next time the person comes in to the Branch.

   Approach the person and hand him/her the Court Order. Be sure you have a backup when you do this.

6. The TRO has a Proof of Service page. When you have served the order you sign and date it, and return it to Headquarters. The Director of Libraries returns it to the City Attorney, who in turn sends it to the Court.

7. Once a TRO has been issued, you are responsible for calling law enforcement should the perpetrator turn up in your Branch. All Branch staff and substitutes should be alerted that they must do this.

8. TROs are for a limited period. The City Attorney, a representative of the Branch, and the Director of Libraries must go to Court to ask for a permanent order. In Court the judge asks the defendant if she/he objects to the order. If the answer is "no," or if the defendant doesn't turn up, the decision in favor is easier. If the defendant answers "yes," the judge's decision will be based on her/his confidence in the credibility of the Library staff.

To Summarize:

30 Day Cooling Off Periods are a useful tool for protecting the staff and the public from harassing members of the public. A temporary restraining order is a last resort action. Remember that both actions, but especially getting a TRO, require documentation. So fill out Incident Reports and write e-mail!

Santa Cruz Public Libraries

NOTICE OF BANNING FROM LIBRARY

You, _____ , are banned from using the _____ Branch Library of

Name of Patron

the Santa Cruz City-County Library System for the next thirty (30) days, because you have broken the following Library rules and

ignored warnings about this behavior. Broken rules:

You may return to the _____ Branch Library on _____ . If you again violate Library rules, the

Date

Library will seek a Restraining Order from the Court banning you from library use for a longer period. You have a right to appeal

this decision within 24-hours to _____ (_____).

Branch Manager/Director of Libraries   Office Phone

_____   _____   _____

Signature of Staff Person   Name of Staff Person   Date

White – Patron   Yellow – Incident Report   Pink – Public Desk   EWA: U/Word Docs/Notice of Banning   9/01

Library Headquarters and System Services
1543 Pacific Avenue • Santa Cruz, California 95060

- -

THEFT OF LIBRARY MATERIALS OR OTHER PROPERTY

1. If the Checkpoint system alarm goes off, say:

   "Excuse me Sir/Ma'am. I think we forgot to check out your materials. Please step back to the desk and I will take care of it.

2. Keep asking for, and charging out, library items until the alarm no longer sounds when the patron steps through.

3. If you have trouble with a patron, get staff backup.

Naturally, stealing library materials or other property is against the law. In legal terms, it is larceny, but as usual with the law, it must be handled very carefully. If we want to accuse someone of larceny, we have to demonstrate that two elements are present at the time we catch him/her:

1. That he/she in fact has the library property, and

2. That she/he intended to steal it.

If both these elements are present, the thief can be detained and arrested. Demonstrating possession isn't difficult. Demonstrating intent is harder.

How to Show Intent to Steal

The most common way to demonstrate intent is to show that the thief concealed the item. However, just because you can't see it, does not legally mean it is concealed. To prove intent by concealment, the item has to be hidden in a place where it would not normally be carried.

> Library materials in a briefcase or backpack do not prove intent, because the patron could claim that she/he inadvertently scooped them up with personal papers.

> Library materials carried under clothing, or wrapped in something (like a jacket) can be used as a demonstration of intent; why would a man carry books under his shirt if he didn't intend to conceal and steal them?

Therefore, What to Do

1. Never assume that a patron leaving the library with uncharged materials intends to steal them. Absent mindedness or misunderstanding of library procedures are both reasonable explanations.

2. Approach people with courtesy, using non-accusatory words that objectify the situation:

> "Excuse me, Sir/Ma'am. I think we missed checking out your materials. Please step back to the desk and I will take care of it."

Or,

> "Excuse me, Sir/Ma'am. Did you forget to check out those items? Here, let me have them and I will do it for you. May I have your library card, please?"

3. If the patron refuses to surrender the material, say "It looks to me like you are trying to take library materials without checking them out. That is against the rules. Please give them to me."

> Use an authoritative tone of voice. Make it clear that you mean business. Experience tells us that this often persuades a patron to hand over the material.

4. If the patron again refuses, say the same thing again, this time adding the information that you will telephone law enforcement.

5. If the patron still refuses to surrender the material, call law enforcement. If the patron tries to leave, do not risk injury to yourself by attempting to detain him/her.

6. Immediately write down a physical description of the patron, and give this to the police when they arrive. If you know the patron's name and address (or can get it from the database), give this to the police too.

7. Fill out an Incident Report, and send it to the Administration Office within 24 hours.

When the Checkpoint Alarm Keeps Sounding

The Checkpoint System alarm is activated by only two things: "preconditioned" library materials, and electronic door-opening cards that use radio devices. So if the alarm continues to sound, and you have checked out the books properly, your object is to get the patron to give up materials she/he has hidden, or produce an electronic access card which is setting off the system.

If you have checked out the materials and the alarm sounds again, say

> "The Checkpoint system is not supposed to alarm for anything but library materials. Please help me find the cause of the alarm so that it can be corrected and will not happen to anyone else."

Ask the patron to walk through the system with their personal belongings, and then to go through minus each of the items (purse, briefcase, etc.).

Once the source is pinpointed, the patron will usually come up with library materials they have stashed away. Take them, thank the patron for his/her cooperation, and explain that the system is to provide better service for everyone.

If the patron does not cooperate, she/he probably is a thief. Follow procedures 4, 5, 6, and 7 above.

The Missing Barcode Scam

Apparently some people believe that it is the barcode in an item that is the security device. He/she therefore tears out the barcode label, and walks through the Checkpoint station with the item completely visible. When the alarm sounds, she/he claims that his/her friend has already checked the item out. This is a little like telling your teacher that the puppy ate your homework.

What to Do

1. Ask the patron for the item, and establish that the barcode has been torn out.
2. Tell the patron that you must keep the item, so that a new barcode can be put in it. Alas, this is all we can do here. But do be sure you get the item from the patron.

VANDALISM AND DESTRUCTIVE BEHAVIOR

1. If the patron appears to be approachable, tell him/her to stop immediately.

2. If the patron does not appear approachable, call law enforcement.

The library staff has a right and duty to protect public property. The California Education Code, Section 19910, covers this. Examples of destructive behavior are:

- Destroying or defacing library materials, including slicing pages from books, periodicals, and newspapers.
- Vandalism of library property, including defacing walls and furniture, damaging facilities (such as rest rooms), breaking windows, etc.

Destructive patrons can be merely careless or thoughtless, or they can be dangerous. The staff person observing the behavior must size up the situation and decide on the best method for handling it.

1. If the patron seems harmless, tell the patron to cease the behavior immediately.

EXAMPLE: [this really happened]

STAFF: Sir, slicing pages out of a library magazine is destroying library property, and is against the rules. Please stop it right now.

PATRON: Hey, it's just an advertisement. That's not destroying property. Anyway, I'm a taxpayer. This belongs to the taxpayers, right?

STAFF: If you cut an advertisement out of a magazine you are interfering with someone else's right to read it. That is why it's considered vandalism, and is against the law.

Report the behavior to the Person in Charge, who should discuss restitution with the offender.

2. If the patron does not appear to be approachable, call law enforcement immediately. The Library will prosecute anyone who maliciously destroys library property, but arrest power can only be exercised when the vandalism has been observed and is committed in the presence of the person signing the citation or making the arrest.

3. In either case, write an Incident Report for your Branch's file. If law enforcement is called, send the Incident Report to the Administration Office within 24 hours.

VERBAL ABUSE OF STAFF

1. Remain calm, and remember to use your Angry or Irate Patron techniques, particularly "Stand and Deliver."

2. Say to the patron:

   "Your language and behavior are not appropriate to the library. You must either stop, or leave right now and come back when you have calmed yourself."

3. Get backup from other staff.

No staff person needs to listen to abusive or obscene language from a library user.

1. Try to remain calm, and remember that you *personally are not the cause* of the patron's inappropriate response or language. The patron would like to make you mad. Don't provide that satisfaction. Instead, use "Stand and Deliver" to wait the patron out.

2. Remember, too, that other patrons are listening to how you handle the situation. They are on your side, and will stay there if you are calm, do not get angry, and act reasonably but firmly.

3. Tell the patron, "Your language and behavior are not appropriate in the library and are causing a disturbance. You must either stop, or leave right now and come back when you have calmed yourself."

4. Other staff should come to support the staff person being abused. The Person in Charge should intervene to try to defuse the situation. Sometimes the best thing to do is just to walk away.

5. If the patron continues to be abusive, do not argue. Say, "You will have to leave the Library right now or I will call for help."

6. If the patron refuses to leave, the Person in Charge or a co-worker should call law enforcement or other community backup.

7. Write an Incident Report for your Branch's file. If a person is injured, property is damaged, or law enforcement is called, send the Incident Report to the Administration Office within 24 hours.

See also ANGRY AND IRATE PATRONS

SANTA CRUZ PUBLIC
L I B R A R I E S   **Incident Report Form**
A City County System

Instructions to Staff Handling Incident: Please fill out this form completely, sign below, and give it to your Branch Manager. Please print clearly.

BRANCH_____ DATE _____ TIME_____

STAFF PRESENT_____

NAME OF PATRON (if known) _____

DESCRIPTION OF INCIDENT _____

_____

DESCRIPTION OF PATRON _____

_____

WITNESSES: (Get phone numbers and addresses if possible) _____

_____

ACTION TAKEN _____

_____

POLICE/FIRE CALLED? Yes [ ] No [ ] TIME_____ TIME ARRIVED _____

CASE NUMBER _____

ADDITIONAL COMMENTS: _____

_____

_____   _____
SIGNATURE (Staff Person Handling Incident)   **DATE**

Instructions to Branch Managers: If the incident involved personal injury to a staff person or member of the public, damage to public property, or law enforcement officials were called, SEND THIS FORM TO THE ADMINISTRATIVE OFFICES LOCATED AT HEADQUARTERS WITHIN 24 HOURS. DO NOT KEEP A COPY. If necessary, the Office Staff will file appropriate risk management reports, attesting that all other records of the incident have been destroyed. If risk management forms are not required, this incident report form will be returned to you for your files.

DESCRIPTION

SEX	RACE	AGE	HEIGHT
HAIR			WEIGHT
EYES			HAT COLOR, TYPE
GLASSES TYPE			COAT
TATTOOS			SHIRT
SCARS/MARKS			TROUSERS
COMPLEXION			SHOES

OTHER DISTINGUISHING CHARACTERISTICS

WHAT THE SUSPECT SAID:

LIBRARY MATERIALS COMMENT FORM

LIBRARY BRANCH:_____**DATE:**_____

AUTHOR: _____

TITLE: _____

PUBLISHER: _____

DATE OF PUBLICATION: _____**CALL NUMBER:** _____

WHAT BROUGHT THIS ITEM TO YOUR ATTENTION? *(REVIEWS, WORD-OF-MOUTH, ETC.)*
_____

IF REVIEWS, PLEASE GIVE THE NAME AND DATE OF PUBLICATIONS, IF POSSIBLE:
_____

HAVE YOU READ/REVIEWED THE ENTIRE ITEM? _____

TO WHAT DO YOU OBJECT? *(PLEASE BE SPECIFIC, CITING PAGES IF POSSIBLE)*
_____

_____
CONTINUE ON REVERSE IF MORE SPACE IS NEEDED

YOUR NAME: _____   _____**PHONE:** _____

COMPLETE ADDRESS:
_____

_____

REPRESENTING SELF? _____

REPRESENTING ORGANIZATION? NAME: _____

_____
SIGNATURE

Appropriate Library Staff will give careful consideration to the points you raise, and will respond in writing as soon as possible.

FOR STAFF USE ONLY

Date Received:	Assigned To:
Date Completed:	
Original to Assistant Director, copy to Branch Manager.	
Copies of complaint and completed response are filed by the Assistant Director.	
1.) To Director 2.) Library Files	

THE LIBRARY RULES

- The public library is open to all. No one has the right to interfere with any-one else's right to use the library.
- No smoking.
- No food or beverages.
- No bicycles in the building.
- No soliciting or panhandling.
- No animals except guide dogs.
- Please speak in soft tones only. Use cell phones outside the building only.
- Backpacks and personal belongings must be kept under tables and chairs.
- Children under 9 years must be supervised by a person 14 years of age or older.
- Library materials and furniture belong to all the people. Please use them with care.

Santa Cruz City County Library System

1543 Pacific Avenue

Santa Cruz, CA 95060

Index